Build Your Own
WOOD-
FIRED
OVEN

Build Your Own
WOOD-
FIRED
OVEN

ALAN WATT

ROSENBERG

First published in Australia in 2011
by Rosenberg Publishing Pty Ltd
PO Box 6125, Dural Delivery Centre NSW 2158
Phone: 61 2 9654 1502 Fax: 61 2 9654 1338
Email: sales@rosenbergpub.com.au
Web: www.rosenbergpub.com.au

Reprinted 2012, 2013, 2015, 2016,
2017, 2019

National Library of Australia Cataloguing-in-Publication data:

Author: Watt, Alan, 1941-

Title: Build your own wood-fired oven / Alan Watt.

ISBN: 9781921719028 (pbk.)

Notes: Includes bibliographical references and index.
Subjects: Stoves, Wood—Design and construction.

Dewey Number: 683.88

Set in 12 on 14 point Myriad Pro
Printed in China through Colorcraft Ltd, Hong Kong

Contents

Acknowledgments

I acknowledge the ongoing support of Fiona Tunnicliff and Alan Gray, editor of *Earth Garden* magazine, in their coverage of the wood-fired oven workshops.

To John Curlis, Greg Daly, Mark Hulme, David Martin, Lee O'Connell, my appreciation for their past and recent specialist technical advice.

I am also indebted to Peter Bell, David Endacott, Dennis O'Hoy, Rob Porkka and Priscilla Wegars for their advice, guidance and expert knowledge in my investigation of stone-built ovens.

To my teenage neighbour, Christian Bond, who was prepared to take on the task of photographing many of the oven construction sequences and rescuing me from the mysteries of computer technology, my thanks.

I am grateful to Jen Mallinson for her artistic input into the cover design; to my colleague, Bernd 'Bernie' Weise, for his contribution to the expansion and refinement of the workshops, and to the many friends, workshop hosts and participants, who have not only allowed me to use their photographs, but in offering such enthusiasm, hospitality and friendly company, have made the workshops more of a social occasion than a mere teaching task.

Finally, to my family, who has seen, yet, another major undertaking (while others remain incomplete) my gratitude for their forbearance, quiet encouragement and acceptance of the time not spent in their company.

Foreword

'Blessed are the wood-fired oven makers, for they will be called children of Alan Watt.'

Does that give you some idea of how much I admire this book and its author? Alan Watt is the doyen of Aussie DIY wood-fired oven builders. He is the guru who has refined his multitude of skills and generously presented all his hard-won knowledge to countless eager oven workshop participants over many years. I was lucky enough to attend one of Alan's weekend oven-making workshops once: it was a wonderful experience that led me to publish three books on the topic.

Alan's book is a treasure trove of ideas, guidance and wisdom. When Alan recommends something – anything – you can be sure his advice is based on years of practical and personal experience. Rarely have I met someone so generous with their knowledge. So here in this book is a comprehensive guide to building your own wood-fired oven. Luckily, Alan writes in a clear and concise way, so I have no doubt that this book will attract legions of fans.

If you've never experienced the sensual joy of biting into a piping hot pizza, or crusty bread, fresh from a hand-built wood-fired oven – this book will let you join the wood-fired oven cooking family. This book is entrée to that world, main course and dessert all rolled into one light but substantial whole. Enjoy.

Alan Gray

Editor, *Earth Garden* magazine

Introduction

Nothing from my Australian family background or cultural heritage would suggest I would become involved in building and using wood-fired ovens, especially in relation to the culinary fare that is most commonly associated with this ancient style of cooking.

Coming from a long line of Anglo-Saxons and living, then, in the 1940s, within a homogeneous society, you could say that our family cuisine, like most other families I knew, was undeniably British – perhaps, in our case, with a little Scottish influence. Although I regarded my mother and grandmothers as being very capable cooks they presented plain meals, with the occasional enhancement of a few herbs and spices such as mint, parsley, chives and sometimes a powdered mustard from a square yellow tin marked 'Keens'.

Meat and three veg seemed a standard for most days, usually served at the evening meal, then known as 'tea'. Lamb or sausages were the common meat component, with occasionally liver or steak and kidney, but Sunday roast usually called for something special like roast beef, or even more special, roast chicken. I cannot recall ever having seen garlic, chilli, rosemary, olives or olive oil on the family table. Olive oil was certainly in the house – but only as part of the medicine chest.

It was not until I attended the Melbourne Teachers' College, to study as an art teacher, in the late 1950s that, along with most fellow students from similar backgrounds, I discovered a cornucopia of exotic foods, the likes of which none of us had come across before. The teachers' college (now part of Melbourne University) was in Carlton, an inner city suburb where, after the large post-war immigration program, many from Mediterranean countries settled, but it was the Italians who really made it their new home and developed numerous businesses around the main thoroughfare, Lygon Street.

Many Italian cafes and restaurants were established along this now famous street, and it was there that my fellow students and I would often go for lunch, clad in duffle coats and desert boots – the unofficial uniform of Melbourne student youth at the time. There, within a couple of blocks of the college, we were in a foreign land and like any tourists indulged in the delights on offer. It was not just coffee we ordered but espresso, cappuccino or latte – all a far cry from the coffee and chicory essence my father became so used to during the war.

And we were not just eating foreign foods, we were talking a foreign language. The once familiar spaghetti and tomato sauce which came precooked in a tin was replaced by 'pasta' – fettuccini, linguini, ravioli and lasagne. At the Greek restaurant we were eating what was for me fried fishing bait (squid and whitebait), and our salads came 'tossed', with olives, tomatoes and feta 'dressed' in olive oil and lemon juice. Whatever happened to shredded lettuce and grated carrot, a shaving of cheddar cheese, a thin circle of staining beetroot and the decorative twirl of a curled slice of orange? And where's the mayonnaise?

But of all these epicurean discoveries the most delightful was PIZZA! Now here was something quite different and special and unless you had been to Italy, or other countries where Italians had long been established, it is unlikely that you would have ever heard of it. In 1961 Toto's pizzeria opened in Lygon Street, claiming to be the first pizza house in Australia (of course, rival city Sydney makes counter-claims). This was the perfect place for a student meal offering a further extension of taste sensations – anchovies, artichoke hearts, pepperoni sausage, capers and a cheese that stretched into fine threads as you took a bite of the wedged-shaped segment. Maybe this was the initial step on the path to becoming involved with wood-fired ovens and the wonderful food they produced.

Having completed three years of art teacher training there was an opportunity for further study as a professional artist and teacher at the Royal Melbourne Institute of Technology, in the heart of the city but not far from familiar Lygon Street.

I had selected to major in ceramic arts, then simply called 'Pottery'. Over the next six years, apart from the common core subjects of art history, life drawing and minor studies in sculpture and painting, I was involved in all the creative and technical aspects of the ceramic medium, from formulating clay bodies and glazes to stacking and firing electric kilns.

At the time there was a growing movement of returning to grass-roots living and many artists and craft practitioners were heading to the 'bush' to build homes of mud brick and recycled building materials and to live a life of 'long hair and bare feet'. This period, within the pottery fraternity, gave rise to a general acceptance, even enthusiasm, for a different approach to the craft, as outlined in a major reference book that combined technical information with a philosophic approach to the making of pottery. *A Potter's Book*, written by the Englishman Bernard Leach in 1940, became a major influence within the English-speaking world over the direction that ceramic art was to take in the next few decades.

While living in Japan, Leach was introduced to pottery making and came under the influenced of prominent personalities, and the philosophies, behind the *mingei* (traditional folk art) movement. His book describes the process of firing kilns to high temperatures with wood, for stoneware and porcelain, and persuasively argues that natural qualities imparted on wood-fired articles are sympathetic with Zen aesthetics. This fitted comfortably with the general trend to return to basics and by the early 1960s a number of Australian potters had been drawn to Japan to work with local potters and embrace both the aesthetics and making processes associated with *mingei*-style pottery.

Many of these potters eventually returned to Australia, bringing with them knowledge and experience of high temperature wood-fired stoneware. Soon numerous wood-fired brick kilns were being built at country studios where wood was plentiful and there was less danger of offending neighbours with the smoke they produced. Gradually these potters adapted their work to local conditions, digging and preparing nearby clay and developing firing techniques that suited local timbers. The results of these firings were highly regarded as having the hallmarks of those qualities and aesthetic values which were currently appreciated at the time – earthy, obviously handmade and individual.

At our art school we were limited to what we regarded as the rather bland and inferior results of electric kilns fired at far lower earthenware temperatures. After much urging we eventually persuaded our head of department, who had come from an industrial background and was unconvinced by the Leachean approach, to allow us to try a high temperature firing at his small rural property – suggesting to him that it would be a good opportunity to clear his block of fallen trees and branches as the kiln would use a considerable amount of fuel.

Despite all our efforts and sixteen hours of continuous firing, trying all manner of stoking techniques, there was no way we were going to reach our hoped-for stoneware temperatures. It was a classic case of the blind leading the blind. Whether it was the kiln design, the stacking arrangement of the work inside the kiln, or the fuel we had selected, it was obvious we needed guidance from someone who knew what they were talking about. We returned to electric firing at the art school knowing that further exploration of wood firing and stoneware was out of the question, and very envious of our Sydney counterparts who seemed to be encouraged to explore this new area of ceramics.

It was sometime during those early student days that I, along with a couple of art school friends, attended a workshop on the building and firing of a simple wood kiln, run by a husband and wife team who were stoneware potters from Sydney and were held in high regard in the pottery fraternity. It was at this workshop that I learned so much regarding sound design principles for efficient wood kilns and the process of managing the fire for maximum heat transfer.

Although the simple updraft kiln we built was not designed for very high temperatures it reached the desired heat in a very short time with the minimum of wood and fuss. The work which emerged from this kiln displayed dramatically the impact of varying kiln atmospheres of a wood firing on the coloured oxides in the glazes. I was so impressed that I duplicated the kiln at home the following weekend.

I can still recall the thrill and excitement of seeing the glazes begin to sinter at red heat and gradually form a glassy surface as the temperature increased and the glow from my simple house-brick kiln intensified to a shimmering, intense orange whiteness. I had fallen for the magic and allure that the mastering of a wood-fired kiln offers. I think I had taken my second step to a future involvement with wood-fired ovens. Over the next forty years I build numerous fuel-burning kilns using wood, oil and gas as part of my own studio practice, and as part of my professional career in teaching ceramic students at tertiary level there was also the supervision of student-built kilns.

After I was appointed to the then Canberra School of Art, we made it a policy to try and take all students, at the beginning of the year, to my coastal property for what we called a 'kiln camp'. Partly this was for social reasons so that the new intake of students would be helped to integrate with students from other years. The other aim was to demystify the process of making ceramics, with its attendant expectation that making ceramics could only be done by using sophisticated materials bought at commercial outlets. Maybe my own experience at art school in the era of hippiedom and self-sufficiency was difficult to shake off.

The students were set the task of making work from the clay found on the property and to construct a kiln in which to fire that work also from materials found nearby. I knew the property contained many different clays and there was a large area of native forest which provided plenty of suitable fallen timber for fuel. Having some experience of firing gas kilns at the art school the senior students were aware of the design considerations in making an efficient high-temperature kiln and set about trying to achieve this with the limited resources available to them.

Over the years many unique kilns were built with varying success, but a kiln built in the bush twenty years ago in the latter years of the kiln camps still remains as a testament to both student ingenuity and the resilience of Mother Earth. This old kiln was built from a mixture of approximately equal parts of clay, from my property, sand from a local source and fine crushed stone that remained in an old roadside dump, courtesy of the local council. The kiln comprises a long throat as a firebox and two downdraft chambers in which to fire the work. It reached a surprising 1300° C (2372° F) after an 18-hour firing with some excellent results in stoneware and porcelain. Despite being exposed to the elements since it was last fired the structure remains sound with some erosion taking place on the outer surfaces.

The structural mixture of clay as a binder, sand to open the clay up to minimise shrinkage and fine stone as an aggregate for strength was to be the recipe I used for the first wood-fired workshop I conducted in 2003. I'm not sure why it took so long for me to build my own first wood-fired oven but for someone who had built, and been associated with building, so many wood-fired kilns it now seems an inexcusable delay for a pizza and wood-fired oven food enthusiast.

With no plans, but some close observations of a few wood-fired ovens at reputable pizza houses and an acquired knowledge of refractory materials I set about building my own wood-fired oven, using castable refractory for the oval-based dome. It seemed obvious to begin with pizza for the first 'firing' and as I had more confidence in building the oven than cooking in it there was a few quick lessons to be learned.

After some early disasters corrections were made and it wasn't long before I thought I had some grasp on the process of managing the temperature and cooking pizzas. With confidence, invitations were offered to friends and neighbours who came to try some dishes from the new oven and before I knew it I was building ovens around the district for these previous enthusiastic visitors.

Eight years ago a neighbour passed on to me an advertisement in a community arts magazine asking for a tutor to run a cob oven weekend workshop, involving the construction of a wood-fired oven, at Coonabarabran, in New South Wales. As I had not been to this town, noted for its numerous astronomy observatories, I thought I should contact the organiser to offer my services. They accepted me as their tutor for the workshop to be held during the town's 'Festival of the Stars'. Cob construction, the method used to make many student kilns at our kiln camps and described in Chapter 4, Building Your Oven from the Earth, would certainly be capable of meeting the temperature demands of a wood-fired oven, I thought. The oven turned out to be a success and while I had no thoughts of further involvement in building wood-fired ovens it became the beginning of dozens of future workshops

When news of this first workshop reached a local community college they asked if I could run a similar workshop on my own property. On the basis of what I had learned from Coonabarabran I suggested that two ovens be made – one a low-tech adobe oven and the other a more permanent high-tech oven made from either brick or castable refractory. It was also important, I felt, that the participants have an opportunity to see one oven in action, so a pizza feast was arranged for the second day of the weekend workshop. While this meant that I had to gradually and slowly remove the sand mould from the low-tech oven well into Saturday night, before inserting a small gas ring into the emptied oven to dry it completely, the effort was worth it, as participants were able to see the fire in action as evidence of what had been described regarding efficient oven design This set the format for the numerous workshops which were to follow.

Having retired from teaching it was not my intention to begin a business of teaching on a private basis, even though this was a related area in which I felt I had some expertise. But as the number of requests for workshops increased, from community groups, schools, clubs and individuals, and as I found the enthusiasm of participants from all walks of life so infectious, and their company enjoyable, I decided to devote a few weekends a year to continue the workshops.

A website was established to outline the nature of the course and to advertise future events, thus beginning a regular round of workshops that fitted around other farming and artistic commitments. As awareness of the workshops spread though the web, magazine articles, television and word of mouth I began to receive queries and requests for information from all parts of Australia and overseas. Many came from very remote places where it was unlikely that I would ever be able to run a workshop, and as this difficulty was conveyed to the prospective workshop participants there was often a request in return for plans and/or instructions on how to build a wood-fired oven.

While I had produced an illustrated colour workshop manual, as both reinforcement for and an extension of the knowledge acquired through the discussions and activities of the weekend, it fell well short of a guide for someone who hadn't attended a workshop. While there are already some good books available on the building of wood-fired ovens, many are specific to one particular type of construction method and others offer plans for ovens that tend to be over-engineered and expensive for the average do-it-yourself builder. These were the motivations for writing this book.

In considering what would be the most important aspects that a distant reader might look for in such a book, I drew on the many questions that arise during workshops and from other queries posed on email. Many of the people who desire to build their own wood-fired oven come from the most remote places so to advise them of materials and equipment that are citycentric in availability immediately crushes enthusiasm and sees the project put into the too-hard basket.

I have attempted to offer the reader/builder a number of different approaches to building a wood-fired oven so that they may make comparisons and find one, or combinations of more than one, that will suit their budget, building capabilities, available materials, site situation and aesthetic sensibilities.

While I have been involved in the construction of scores of ovens of all different types, at workshops and privately, never have two identical ovens resulted. Although each has its individual characteristics their commonality is an adherence to sound principles of wood oven design, and as a result most people are happy with the results. I have tried to avoid 'absolutes' so that the reader/builder can make choices of size, style, materials and construction methods. As long as there is an understanding of what each component of the oven is intended to perform, and is built to meet those needs efficiently, then there can be great flexibility.

Many people hesitate to take on the building a wood-fired oven not because they want to avoid the task of building but simply because they do not know what to build. I hope this book helps.

Alan Watt
Tanja, Australia
2011

1   A Brief History of Wood-fired Ovens

The history of baking began when Neolithic people gathered grains and after grinding them into flour either made a paste that could be poured over a heated flat rock or made a dough and placed it in the embers of a fire.

An example of the use of an enclosure that retained heat to be transferred to the dough can be found from the Old Kingdom of Egypt (beginning about 3000 BC) where thick pottery moulds, filled with the dough, were placed on the embers to cook. By the time of the Middle Kingdom, conical cones were placed over the dough on a hot hearth and the dough baked by radiant heat.

From the later New Kingdom (16th – 11th centuries BC) we see in a pictogram images of a royal bakery where the baker is slapping dough against the inner wall of an open-topped conical clay cylinder. The dough adheres

Pictogram of bread baking from the tomb of Ramesses III. Valley of the Kings, 11th century BC.

surface of the oven and is peeled off once cooked. Similar examples have been found in ancient Mesopotamia and the Indus Valley. Contemporary versions of this kind of oven are the Indian tandoori ovens and the bread ovens of Uzbekistan.

The first front-loaded ovens, in which a variety of bread styles were baked, are attributed to ancient Greece. It was in Greece that baking in ovens became a trade and specialist bakers sold their products to the public. A unique form of oven also developed in Greece was the portable oven – a small open-mouthed pottery enclosure that was heated from beneath so that the radiant heat cooked the food within.

Ancient Greek portable oven, 17th century BC

The Romans continued the use of the front-loading ovens and it is in Pompeii that we find clear evidence of the existence of a lively baking trade. About thirty-five bakeries have been identified in Pompeii. The largest operations normally had their own mills for grinding the grain. One of the ovens that has been unearthed contained 85 loaves, indicating large-scale production; local distribution from each bakery would have been common.

Two of the many brick-constructed ovens from ancient Pompeii, Italy.

The origins of a pizza-style flatbread covered with different edible ingredients are somewhat obscure, although it is known that the ancient Greeks and Romans ate flat round bread with an assortment of toppings. Marcus Porcius Cato (234–139 BC) wrote in his history of Rome of 'a flat round of dough dressed with olive oil, herbs and honey baked on stone'.

In 1552 tomatoes were introduced to Italy from the New World (actually from Peru) and the poor people, and especially the sailors, of Naples started to include them, along with olive oil, garlic and herbs, on a yeast dough baked in an oven. This particular form of pizza became extremely popular and in honour of its strong connection with sailors (*marinari*) became known as *pizza marinara*. The traditional *pizza marinara* contained no seafood, unlike many modern versions, and for hundreds of years was sold by street vendors. The modern pizzeria is believed to have begun in 1830 in Naples with the opening of Antica Pizzeria Port'Alba, a restaurant where people could sit down to eat their pizza.

In 1889 Don Raffaele Esposito, a well-known Neapolitan *pizzaiolo* (pizza chef), was invited by the King of Italy to his palace to cook his specialties for the royal family. Of the three styles of pizza he prepared, one was made from a combination of tomatoes, basil and mozzarella – representing the red, green and white of the Italian flag. The queen, Margherita di Savoia, was so impressed that she wrote to Don Esposito expressing her gratitude. The recipe was dedicated to the queen as *pizza margherita*, and remains one of the classic favourites today.

As the ancient Roman Empire spread far and wide so too did the 'Roman oven', of the style unearthed in Pompeii, with evidence of such ovens in numerous outposts of the empire. In turn, as former Roman-occupied countries, such as Spain, began to establish outposts and colonies through invasion or religious missions, so also did the knowledge of baking in dome ovens spread. The Pueblo Indian adobe ovens or *hornos* of New Mexico and related regions are classic examples.

Typical Pueblo Indian clay-based built ovens.

Ovens based on the Roman plan spread throughout Europe, and in most villages and towns communal ovens were established where inhabitants could take their bread and other dishes for baking by the official baker. Many had a wooden board hanging nearby where a roster of baking procedures could be written. These ovens were often sited next to village laundries so one can imagine that they became hubs for social exchange and gossip. In most cases the ovens were owned by feudal lords, other nobility or the church and there was a system of payments to the oven master for services rendered.

In France the communal oven was called a *four banal* (common oven). The oven master or official baker (*fournier*) was recognised as the owner of the oven's heat, and after bread baking was complete he had the right to 'sell' the heat for other purposes such as drying fruits or firewood. A set of established rules forbade the drying of some crops, determined purchasing rights to collect the ashes for fertiliser and even the breadcrumb sweepings for poultry feed.

In some parts of France it was forbidden to own a private oven other than a *four petit* (small oven) that would fit under the chimney-hood of the kitchen fireplace. This was largely to minimise the risk of fire starting in the thatched cottages but may also be seen as supporting a small monopoly.

A *four banal* at Urval, Dordogne, France.

The use of communal ovens eventually spread to the French colonies, particularly Quebec, but without the feudal monopoly. After the French Revolution the communal ovens gradually became public property and in some parts remained in use until after the Second World War,

The communal oven did not catch on in Britain as it did in continental Europe. Some small shops with internal ovens sold bread and buns to the public, but most baking was done in private homes.

A good example of a shop which sold to the public can be found in Bath, England, where in 1680 a young French refugee, Sally Lunn, established a bun shop in what is now Bath's oldest building. The oven was originally fired with faggots of wood within the oven but at a later period an external firebox was incorporated so that there was no need to clean out the ashes from the floor of the oven. It remains open to the public.

Sally Lunn's bun oven in the historic town of Bath. Sally Lunn's Museum Kitchen remains open to the public today.

There are still many houses and cottages in Britain, some hundreds of years old, which contained a small oven built within their fireplace and chimney structures. Some have a flue outlet at the back of the oven which leads to the main chimney while others are built within the large kitchen fireplace. The smoke which would have spilled from the front of the open-mouthed oven was drawn into the large kitchen chimney.

The Industrial Revolution led to the invention of commercial sized ovens – the so-called 'Scotch oven' – with factory-made cast-iron facades and doors, sold for distribution to towns and villages both locally and for export. The factory-made components were incorporated into the structure of large brick

A hearth oven set deep in the large chimney recess of an early nineteenth-century stone cottage, Long Compton, England. The oven, measuring 1150 mm long, 980 mm wide and 400 mm high (45 x 38 x 16 inches), has no chimney, the smoke from the oven would have spilled out from the open door and been gathered by the draw of the major kitchen chimney.

ovens constructed from locally available materials. Many of these ovens were heated from an external firebox, to one side of the oven door, eliminating the need for clearing the floor of coals and ash. Scotch ovens became widely distributed throughout Britain and the colonies, allowing community bakers to supply a large range of breads on a daily basis.

Most community ovens went out of use when large industrial bakeries began wide-scale distribution of their products, their demise often hastened by their purchase by such companies in order to eliminate competition. Other village bakeries simply closed up, with some ovens being demolished for their bricks. In Australia, of the few remaining Scotch ovens that were not demolished or destroyed for other commercial development, some have been re-established and brought back to life as boutique bakeries. They are enjoying

The interior and door of the 1892-built Scotch oven at Trentham in Victoria. The bakery, closed in 1987, was resurrected as Red Beard Bakery in 2005 by a group of young bakers with an enthusiasm for time-honoured artisan bread.

a great deal of patronage as the public rediscovers the delightful qualities of unique artisan breads.

On rural Australian properties where the distance from a town or village

A bread oven at the rear of a chimney of a cottage on the historic Woolmers Estate, established in 1817 at Longford in Tasmania.

made purchasing bread difficult and uneconomic, home baking was continued, either in the large cast-iron stove in the kitchen or in an oven incorporated in the outer wall of the fireplace chimney.

In recent times there has been an upsurge of interest in the building or purchasing of a home backyard oven, largely because of the popularity of pizza, and it is not uncommon to find in a family's outdoor entertaining area a domed oven as a companion to the barbecue.

A wood-fired oven adjacent to a barbecue completes an outdoor entertaining area.

2   Design Considerations

In making a wood-fired oven it is the design aspects which are of critical importance if optimum outcomes and efficiencies are to be achieved.

Deciding on the shape of the oven

Wood-fired ovens are generally of two shapes – a domed form, often referred to as a Roman or Pompeii oven, or a barrel arch construction. There are, of course, tandoori ovens, which are simple updraft cone-shaped ovens, used for cooking Indian food, as well as commercial, under-floor heated pizza ovens, where the cooking space is within a muffle-box that is, in reality, not much different to a standard wood-fired stove. These latter two are outside the present discussion of wood-fired oven design.

The basic difference between the domed shape and a barrel arch is that the former is designed around the nature of flames and the latter around the shape of a brick and the convenience of the bricklayer. My observations and experience suggests that the domed shape is the better of the two when it comes to pizza cooking or when the fire is kept burning during the cooking process. For the baking of breads, roasts and other dishes, where the fire or coals are removed, the difference is less critical.

The barrel arch oven usually comprises a semi-circular arch that sits on two parallel short walls, with a flat vertical back wall and a similar front wall with a smaller arched opening for the door. Some are designed with a slope from the front towards the door, which encourages a downdraft effect on the flames, resulting in better heat retention. Flames from combustion of the fuel will be drawn to the flue by the convection effect caused by heated air rising in the oven-chamber and in the flue. Uneven heating may occur if the hot gases from the fire are not evenly distributed across the ceiling, around the walls and across the floor of the oven. The domed oven accommodates a more even heat distribution than the 'box' nature of a barrel arch oven.

Removal of the fire and coals, thus terminating combustion, as for bread baking or roasting, results in heating being mainly by conduction and radiation from the oven structure. This will result in a more uniform temperature distribution throughout the chamber, with the door closed, especially if the oven is given time to 'soak up heat' before baking or roasting begins'.

I have even seen some arch-shaped wood-fired oven kits based on a catenary arch (the inverted shape of the curve created by hanging a chain between two points). Such an arch is a wonderfully solid structure that has no outward thrust and is ideal if you are building bridges or cathedrals as did Antonio Gaudi) but is not suitable for wood-fired ovens. Basically, the catenary arch is too high to achieve optimum radiation, added to which the door opening has to be equally high to create a satisfactory draw and exiting of gases through the door opening.

It should be noted that when it comes to radiation the height of the oven ceiling is of particular importance. If it is too high, the effect of radiant heat on the food, which is generally cooked at floor level, will be minimised.

Oven shapes: from left to right, dome oven, barrel arch oven and catenary arch oven.

Many domed ovens are circular in floor plan, and semi-circular in elevation, largely because of the construction method of using a fixed gauge from a central point – a trammel – when laying the bricks. For a large oven this method can produce a dome that is excessively high. A lower profile can be achieved by using a telescopic trammel whereby each row of bricks has a slightly lesser radius than the preceding row, but the floor plan is still circular.

A slightly 'oblong' floor plan is superior to a circular plan. A slight swelling towards the back of the oven and a

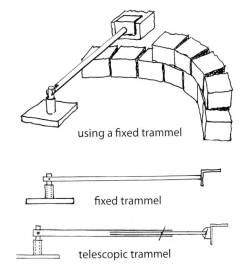

using a fixed trammel

fixed trammel

telescopic trammel

Types of trammel.

narrowing towards the doorway, in both plan and elevation, is even better – see the diagram of the Quebec clay oven. This 'half-avocado' shape encourages a long flame path across the dome towards the door, with the downward pull towards the exit ensuring the retention of heat within the oven. This shape is similar to the sloping-floored *anagama* kiln of Japan, where the kiln is fired at the larger (deeper) end and the heat is drawn to the smaller constricted end before entering the chimney.

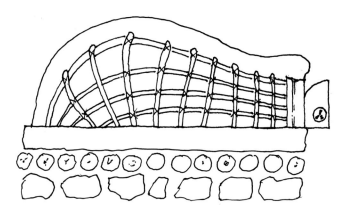

Typical construction of a Quebec clay oven using a wicker of hazel or alder over which the thermal clay mass is built.

The half-avocado shape limits the available cooking area, and in general a compromise is achieved by using a regular oval floor plan or even a somewhat 'squared-off' oval. To achieve irregular shapes like this either a sand mould is used, especially for a cast dome, or a movable profile is positioned on the inner surface of the dome when the bricks are being positioned.

Another drawback of using a centrally positioned trammel is that the dome shape usually begins at ground level, thus creating a a inward sloping angle where the dome meets the floor. This makes it awkward to use cleaning tools, such as a brass broom or coal pushers, effectively, leaving ash and other debris behind.

I am in favour of beginning the dome on a short vertical wall that allows access into the corner and gives greater usable space for containers such as casserole dishes and bread tins. For an example of a dome on a short wall, see Chapter 5, Building Your Oven from Brick.

While the outside form of many ovens reflects the shape of the inner thermal layer, there are many other ovens enclosed within a boxed or circular surround, usually containing loose insulation, which has little bearing on the oven shape within.

Important door/oven height relationship

One of the most important aspects of a good wood-fired oven design is the relationship between the height of the inside of the oven and the height of the oven door or opening. This has an enormous bearing on the optimum efficiency of the oven and therefore on the ease of heating it and the amount of fuel used.

Many books on wood-fired ovens quote a definitive measurement of the door height as 63 per cent of the internal height of the oven. This proportion appears to have its origin in the detailed and thorough research of particular clay-built ovens in rural Quebec, Canada, conducted by Lise Boily and Jean-François Blanchette in 1979, and published in their book *The Bread Ovens of Quebec*. Many subsequent books have perpetuated this proportion of 63 per cent as almost an absolute, but fail to point out that this was an *average* of the measurements taken of many ovens, some of which had a door height to inside dome height proportion of as low as 44 per cent and others as high as 87 per cent. It should be noted, however, that all the ovens appear to have had a standard hinged, double metal door opening of roughly semi-circular shape and were without chimneys.

A number of factors have a bearing on the optimum proportion of the door/inside dome relationship. If you compare a broad rectangular post-and-lintel opening to a high arched opening, there is the obvious ease with which hot gases can escape through the width of a broad opening when compared to the restrictive area presented by a high arch. If there is an external chimney involved, especially a tall chimney that perhaps exits through a roof structure, an amount of 'pull' or draw on the exiting gases once the chimney reaches optimum heat must be taken into consideration. An internal chimney, on the other hand, has considerable draw, an

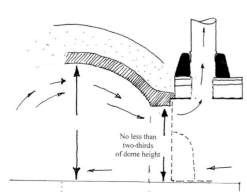

Oven with external flue.

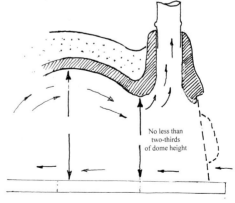

Oven with internal flue.

effect which alters the door/ceiling ratio substantially. In this case the proportion of internal oven height to exit point height is the main consideration, as door height is no longer the exit point for hot gases.

My experience suggests that if the exit point for escaping gases, be it the oven doorway or base of an internal chimney, is about two-thirds the internal height of the oven, the oven should work well. See the accompanying diagrams. If the exit point on an external chimney is too high much heat is lost through the opening; if the exit point is too low, or restricted, it retards the flow of air into the oven and combustion of wood is made difficult.

No matter how wide the door opening, or the proportion of door area to oven volume, it is the height of the doorway to the internal height of the oven that is of most importance.

A good example of an excessively wide doorway, or opening, occurs in the wood-fired bagel oven illustrated. Because the bagel baker uses the full width of the oven for cooking, the oven opening must extend from one side of the oven to the other.

Andy uses almost the full width of the oven opening in a Montreal bagel bakery.

The oven chimney (if it has one)

A wood-fired oven based on the door/oven height relationship discussed above will work quite successfully without a chimney, provided the wood is satisfactory and the oven chamber is not excessively overloaded with fuel. There are many examples of ovens without chimneys, such as the *hornos* ovens of the Pueblo Indians and the ovens of rural Quebec discussed earlier. Both types of oven are generally outdoors and used mainly for bread. As they are not used for open flame cooking there is no need for the oven to be attended for other than short periods of time.

It is when the oven requires constant attention, as does a pizza oven, that the hot gases emerging from the doorway at face level can produce an uncomfortable situation. The addition of a chimney in this case can direct the escaping gases away from the front of the oven. If the oven is in an enclosed building this is even more important, to remove any smoke and hot gases to the exterior.

On more than one occasion I've been asked at a workshop 'Is it really necessary to have the chimney at the front?', to which my reply has been 'No, but you will have a far less efficient oven if it is elsewhere'. On asking one questioner why he was concerned about the chimney being at the door end, he replied, 'It doesn't look natural at the front'. I could only conclude that either he was a steam train buff or was so used to wood stoves that seeing a chimney anywhere than at the end opposite to the fire was quite odd.

It is the drawing of the heat over the oven ceiling, from the fire at the back and downwards towards the exit point near the door, that makes for efficient and even heat distribution and retention. That said, there are ovens that have a chimney or exit point at the 'back' while the fire is positioned towards the front or doorway. These ovens were generally set into the fireplace areas in houses built during the seventeenth to nineteenth centuries and the exiting gases connected with the kitchen's main chimney, and were used exclusively for baking after the coals had been removed from the oven. It would be impossible to conduct any open-flame cooking under such conditions

When discussing the position of chimneys at one workshop, I was alerted to the fact that celebrity chef Jamie Oliver had a large hemispherical wood-fired oven with the chimney positioned in the centre. I was startled by this construction. Only when I did an internet search did I find that Jamie's oven actually had a much lower profile than a hemisphere and was covered by a second brick structure in the form of a full hemisphere. The oven gases were not being extracted through a central chimney but were drawn to the front of the oven, as in a conventional oven, and then into a ducted metal pipe which was directed over the top of the oven, beneath the outer skin, to the central chimney.

I have built only one such oven myself, on an occasion when a friend asked me to site the oven prior to the building of a covered area taking place. The bricklayer positioned the oven base and the carpenter built the high open-sided roof structure above. When I came to build the oven I found the optimal chimney position directly below a large structural beam, so it was necessary to make a channel within the dome structure and direct the exiting gases to a point where the chimney could safely pass through the roof, missing the beam.

A similar oven was built during a workshop where the host, who ran an accommodation establishment, wanted his oven partly covered by a verandah so guests would not get wet when it rained.

In both cases the same result could have been achieved by creating elbows and bends in the chimney to bypass the obstacles, but aesthetic considerations demanded otherwise.

There seems endless discussions about the merits or otherwise of the chimney position being outside the doorway, as in typical pizza ovens, or within the oven. With clay-based ovens it is often difficult to build the complicated arrangement for an outside flue with such fragile material, and consequently the chimney exit point is usually from within.

I can honestly say that after having built and fired dozens and dozens of ovens, of brick, adobe and castable, with chimneys in both positions, I have found little difference in their operation, provided – and this is most important – that the inside chimney exit point is as forward as possible (just behind the door opening), and almost as low as the top of the doorway so there is a downwards pull on the gases, and there must be some form of damper to control the loss of heat from the oven. Rarely do you see some form of damper on an internal chimney arrangement, however. I know this will rankle the traditional pizza oven purists, but that is my observation and experience from over a hundred wood-fired oven workshops and more than fifty years' experience in managing fuel-burning kilns.

There is generally no need for a damper to be incorporated in a chimney which is on the outside of the doorway as it does not have the same draw on the oven gases as an internal chimney. In fact, some air can also be drawn into the chimney from outside, especially when the fire is low and does not have a large volume of hot gases flowing up the chimney. There are instances, especially when the chimney must be of excessive length to exit a building, where a damper might be introduced to slow the draw.

The calculations determining the diameter (or internal area) and length of a chimney are complicated, but relate to the volume and floor area of the oven chamber, the length of horizontal and downward pull of the gases to exit the oven, and the heat the chimney is likely to reach in operation. The chimney is said to reach optimum efficiency at 150° C (300° F). While I have attempted to find some formula that would assist the oven builder in this matter, it appears that there is no simple answer to cover the variations that different oven designs present. In the three chapters on building ovens you will see I have given specific sizes for the chimneys in the instructions, but those measurements are based more on intuition, from long experience, than any calculation of formulae.

I can only offer one word of advice – it is easier to make a chimney larger than you think you need and have the ability to damper it down than make it too small and have no way of opening it up.

Under the oven floor options

While a wood-fired oven can be built on a large variety of base structures, it is the area immediately under the oven floor that should be given serious consideration, depending mainly on how you wish to use your oven. The two main options are to have a well-insulated subfloor where the heat retained in the oven, and particularly the floor (hearth, sole), is kept from dissipating, or some form of heat sink (heat bank) where the heat can be stored to 'give back' to the oven after the fire has been removed. In the former case less fuel and time are required to build the heat up to cooking temperatures, but less residual heat remains beneath the floor for long-term baking when the fire is removed. Such an arrangement is ideal for pizza and open-flame cooking where the continuing fire can keep the heat spread throughout the oven.

A number of insulation materials can be used under the floor, but avoid soft and loose materials as these do not give a solid foundation on which a satisfactory floor can be built. Insulation materials such as insulating fire bricks, CalSil board (a calcium/silicate firm board), ceramic fibre board (but not soft blanket), autoclaved aerated concrete blocks (AAC), often referred to by their trade names (Hebel, Xella, Eco), a setting wet mix of either vermiculite or perlite with high temperature cement (6:1), or, if it is not likely to become too hot, with regular Portland cement. If you choose to lay down a level of setting mixture, the cement or binder component should be *just* enough to form a firm base, for the denser the mix the less insulation properties it will have. With a subfloor of insulation material the heat will be retained in the dense material used for the actual floor, and its thickness will also determine heat-retention time.

Many commercial oven marketers extol the virtue of their ovens being capable of heating up, ready for cooking, in a very short time – but you can guarantee that there will be an equally rapid cooling if the heat is not kept up to their thin thermal layers.

The alternative approach is to create a thick layer of dense material beneath the floor which will slowly absorb the heat from the oven and the floor and which, when the fire has been removed, will act as a heat bank and contribute to the conductive heat-holding capacity of the floor for long and steady heat delivery. Of course the time it takes to heat the oven to working temperatures is longer and the fuel use is greater, but it will provide steady heat for much longer, especially if overnight roasts or multiple bread loadings are to be considered.

Suitable dense materials include solid brick, poured high-temperature castable or solidly packed decomposed granite or gravel (as long as it has enough clay content to pack firm and set hard). Avoid loose sand or soft fill as these provide insufficient firmness for a stable floor. The heat bank material can be contained in a well beneath the oven floor. To stop the flow of any heat dissipating from the mass, the well can be lined with insulating material as described above.

Insulating materials

Like any good real estate agent I can only stress 'Insulate! Insulate! Insulate!'

Considering the effort oven-builders go to in forming a good solid thermal mass around the oven chamber, it seems a great pity that all too often their efforts are not maximised by surrounding that thermal layer with substantial insulation. There also seems some confusion about what creates insulation – I have often heard the mud and sand covering an oven being referred to as an insulation layer when in fact they are the opposite, just more thermal mass.

It was common practice in village bakeries to cover the ovens with (and site them on) massive amounts of sand or other heat-holding materials, in order to retain as much heat as possible so that little fuel would be required to bring the temperature up for the next day's baking. As these ovens were only allowed to cool down if repairs were required they would ordinarily be constantly warm for every day of the year. One old Scotch bread oven in Australia, built about 1850, was found to be in need of repair soon after it was brought back into use a few years ago. After waiting many days for the oven to cool enough to begin work, the modern-day bakers had to remove about 7 tonnes of sand from the top of the oven to access the brickwork.

An oven that is used only intermittently requires the heating of the thermal mass from cold, and the thicker the mass the longer it takes to heat. The heat will be retained longer with the use of thicker, quality insulation.

A number of materials can be used for insulating ovens, some of which have been mentioned earlier, but the common characteristic of all insulating materials is that they contain tiny pockets of air spaces, some microscopic,

A commercially built oven contained within a galvanised iron water tank.

A boxed enclosed oven built with great skill by a former workshop participant.

which prevent the ready transfer of heat through the material.

In earlier times materials such as charcoal, sawdust, coke, ash, straw (mixed with a binder such as mud) were used, as long as they were not close enough to hot surfaces to burn. In contemporary times insulating firebricks, vermiculite, perlite, AAC blocks and ceramic fibre (developed by NASA for protecting the re-entry of rockets into Earth's atmosphere) have largely replaced them.

For ovens that are built within a brick or metal enclosure loose materials such as vermiculite or perlite can simply be poured into the cavity surrounding the oven, and the enclosure capped to keep out rain and prevent the light, loose material from blowing away.

Where a dome-shaped oven is to be insulated it is necessary to combine loose insulation materials with some form of binder so that it can be trowelled over the thermal mass. High-alumina cement or Portland cement are commonly used for brick or cast ovens, and clay for low-tech adobe ovens. It is important when using a binder to hold together loose materials that only the minimum amount be used, for as the density of the mix increases its insulating properties decrease.

For low-tech adobe ovens it is common to use readily available cheap materials in the insulation layer. See Chapter 4, Building Your Oven from the Earth. Chopped straw, charcoal or sawdust mixed with a little clay will help insulate the thermal layer, as will cow dung, which is mostly fibrous material. I suspect many other materials that are light and contain tiny pockets of air should work and I have often contemplated trying, at one of the workshops, clay mixed with rice bubbles, popcorn, pumice or cellulose packing pellets. Avoid products like styrene foam pellets, though, as they can give off toxic fumes when they get hot enough.

Ceramic blanket for a high-tech oven needs to be wrapped over the oven before being capped in a concrete covering. See photos in Chapter 5, Building Your Oven from Brick.

3   Starting Your Wood-fired Oven-building Project

Before you begin the more exciting aspect of actually building your oven, you will need to decide on where it might best be sited and what form of foundation and base would be most appropriate.

While some town councils may have restrictions or regulations on what you can build and where, generally speaking, household outdoor wood-fired ovens are usually covered by the same conditions for building outdoor wood-fired barbecues. You may need to check with your local authority.

The first step in choosing a site is to take into consideration how your oven might be used in the future – whether simply for personal family use or for large social gatherings which will require a larger open space around the oven. It is surprising what a magnet an oven can be with the glow of open-flame cooking in process.

Take into account the prevailing wind conditions (you don't want any smoke in the light-up stage causing irritation to you or your neighbours). Closeness to facilities such as kitchen, dining area, electricity and lighting, rain shelter and wood storage location are all worth taking account of before you start building.

Your next decision is what size oven and type of base is most appropriate for your needs, your budget, your building capabilities and your aesthetic sensibilities. An oven can be built on an already existing structure, but it should be remembered that there is considerable weight in most ovens and an existing structure may require reinforcement.

Most ovens are built on a concrete foundation but if your site is rocky you may not need to add further support. In most cases a 100 mm (4 in) slab of reinforced concrete, extending a little beyond the base of the oven, will be adequate. In colder areas you need to consider the frost line and the risk of frost heave; if frost heave is a concern, the foundation would need to be appropriately stronger.

The base on which the oven sits can be made from many materials. Masonry blocks and bricks are most common, but I have also seen ovens built on sections of large up-ended concrete pipes, rock-built structures, stout timber poles and fabricated steel frames.

On a naturally sloping site there may be an opportunity to terrace the slope and build onto the ground directly, although this would require the use of a waterproof membrane, a concrete base and insulation.

A base of recycled house bricks matches the double skin dome.

Base of irregular local stone.

A terraced bank provides a suitable base.

A masonry block base bagged with cement render.

Here a single massive rock is used as a base.   Fabricated steel frame base.

The height of the oven floor really depends on the height of the people most likely to use the oven, but remember you should have no difficulty in seeing the whole floor of the chamber, especially if you are cooking pizzas or other open-flame dishes. A height of anywhere between 850 mm (33 in) and 1050 mm (41 in) will suit most people.

If you feel that a ledge in front of and surrounding the oven would be advantageous for placing food or as a working surface, then you will need to add that to the dimensions of the oven you decide on.

I often get asked 'What is a convenient size for a home wood-fired oven?' or 'How many pizzas will that size oven cook?' Both questions are difficult to answer – but I would caution against building a monster of an oven simply to cook as many pizzas as possible in the shortest possible time. You will find you have an empty oven with plenty of residual heat going to waste. A monster oven also takes longer to heat up and uses much more fuel than a more modest sized oven.

In the following pages you will see the process of building a number of different types of wood-fired oven. Be aware that they are not mutually exclusive and that there is plenty of scope for combining aspects of the various types to suit your needs and the availability of materials. As long as you are aware of what each component of the building process is attempting to achieve, and you follow the sound design principles that are common to all, there is great flexibility to be had in modifying the construction stages to suit your particular situation.

4   *Building an Oven from the Earth*

Ovens built from the earth have a history that goes back to the earliest times of baking bread, but because such ovens are of a fragile and temporary nature most of our knowledge of them comes via pictograms from early civilisations. The fact that they still exist today, in so many parts of the world, attests to their suitability to produce quality food, although they may be seen as primitive by modern standards. The bread ovens of the Pueblo Indians of North America and the rural ovens of Quebec, Canada, are classic examples.

Quebec oven. Courtesy Canadian Museum of Civilizations. Lise Boily-Blanchette. S 74-12438.

Woman beside an outdoor clay oven in rural Quebec, 1906. Courtesy Canadian Museum of Civilizations. Frank Oliver Call, Fonds Marius Barbeau. PR 2002-60.

Clay-based mixtures, whether called adobe, cob or mud, are much the same, as it is basically a blend of clay material, for strength and workability, with non-plastic components such as sand, silt or loam to 'open' up the clay to prevent excessive shrinkage and therefore cracking.

Clay-based oven

The clay-based oven you are about to follow through various construction stages is typical of what is built during the two-day workshops; what I call a low-tech oven. In this case it is being built on a fabricated frame, but it could just as easily have been built on the ground, on a constructed elevated base or on a terraced bank. The low-tech oven is one of at least two ovens built during the workshops and is normally the one removed from the site at the end of the workshop. Considering the weight that has to be lifted onto some form of transport, this oven is built on an insulation bed to minimise weight, but that is certainly not the only option.

Step 1: Laying a bed of insulation

Laying aerated concrete blocks for insulation.

In this case autoclaved aerated concrete blocks (AAC), known in Australia as Hebel or Eco blocks, in the UK and North America as Xella blocks, have been chosen because of their cheapness, lightness and suitability to withstand the heat such an oven is likely to produce. More expensive alternatives are insulating firebricks, CalSil board or a poured slab made from vermiculite and cement.

The fabricated frame, measuring 1000 x 1200 mm (39 x 47 in), has been designed around the module of the AAC block to eliminate the need for cutting them (although they are soft enough to cut with a handsaw). The oven can be made to larger dimensions but it is easier to base the size of the insulation layer on standard block modules.

The blocks are laid dry to a flat surface. Should any high spots be evident they can easily be rubbed flat with a regular housebrick.

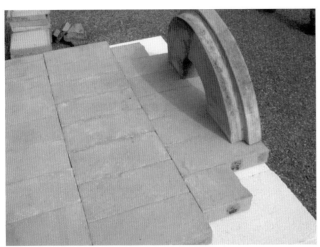

Two views of oven floor of fired clay pavers with particle board door mould in position.

Step 2: Laying the floor of the oven

The floor (hearth, sole) of the oven in this case is to be made from 50 mm (2 in) thick fired clay (ceramic) pavers. Because the top surfaces of most pavers have a bevelled edge or pencil-round edges, place the pavers upside down so that the sharp straight edges of the bottom surfaces fit closely together. Dry-pressed pavers have smoother surfaces than those that are extruded or wire cut. If dry-pressed pavers are unavailable, look for pavers with the least-textured lower surface. If you desire a floor with greater heat-holding qualities, select a thicker paver or a suitable brick.

The door mould you see in the photo is made from two semi-circular pieces of particleboard (MDF) each 32 mm (1¼ in) thick. Plywood can also be used. The larger semicircle has a radius of 28 cm (11 in), the smaller one a radius of 25 cm (10 in). This size can be altered to suit your needs. The two pieces are glued or screwed together to form the mould for what will become a rebated door opening for the oven. A ready source for such material are the waste pieces from kitchen sink or bench top 'cut-outs', available from most joinery shops as scrap.

The first row of pavers is centrally positioned against the front edge of the insulation blocks to cover the width of the door mould. Using a staggered bond layout, the pavers can be laid to form an oval pattern across the rectangular insulator block floor, keeping clear of the other three sides of the insulation layer by approximately 50 mm (2 in). Half or cut pavers are necessary to complete a more oval layout. At this stage the pavers can be bonded to the insulation blocks with air-setting mortar or, if you want to stay as low-tech as possible,, they can be laid on a thin bed of slurry (1 part clay: 3 parts fine sand).

Step 3: Positioning a 'skirt' or short vertical wall on the oven perimeter

The idea behind having a perimeter of pavers on edge is both to protect the lower section of the dome from abrasive wear from wood being thrown against the walls, and to create a short hard vertical surface against which a brass broom or coal pusher can be used to clean right up to the sloping edge of the dome without

The door mould in position on the clay paver oven floor.

damaging the clay-built structure.

The pavers, on edge and with the sharp-edged bottom surfaces facing inwards, begin at the outer edge of what will become the door rebate and form an oval, keeping at least a distance of 112 mm (4½ in) between the inner walls of the pavers and the outside edge of the insulation base. This allows enough room for both the 'hot face' of the thermal layer and the thickness of the insulation.

By manoeuvring the pavers into position 'dry' you should be able to form an oval shape without having to cut any of them. Mark their placement and then bond them to the floor and each other with air-set mortar or clay slurry.

Any small gaps or rough surfaces on the floor can be filled with a thin coating of air-set mortar at the same time.

Sodium silicate-based air-set mortar is only good for thin joints so don't try to fill large gaps with it. As it dries quickly it is important to sponge off any residue with water before it sets.

Laying pavers on edge to form a 'skirt'.

Step 4: Adding a buttress to the paver 'skirt'

A temporary external buttress adds to the strength of the 'skirt'.

This step is not absolutory necessary but it performs three functions. Firstly, it gives backup support to the paver perimeter 'skirt' as sand is packed inside the oval perimeter to form a sand mould. (This becomes particularly important during speed construction of the low-tech oven during a two-day workshop.) Secondly, it gives an extra thickness of thermal mass that enables the oven to retain more heat, and thirdly, it helps to begin the curved shape of the oven dome.

As the buttress is only required to provide temporary support until the dome is formed, it is not necessary to use high-temperature cement; in keeping with the low-tech nature of construction a weak Portland cement-based concrete will suffice. A clay-based mix is also satisfactory if you have time to allow it to become firm.

The photo shows the application of a narrow buttress comprising 4 parts fine crushed stone (stone dust or crusher dust), 2 parts sand, 1 part ordinary builder's cement (Portland).

Step 5: Forming the sand mould

Shaping the sand mould for the oven dome

The best sand to use for making a mould is brickies sand, as used by bricklayers. It is said to be 'fatty', meaning that it contains enough clay to make it bind together, and is easily shaped.

Place the door mould in a central position on the front edge of the paver floor, with a slight backwards lean. It will need to be propped in place with three lengths of timber that will take the weight of the sand (one positioned top centre, the others at the bottom corners).Three projecting screws in the mould will provide anchor points for the supporting props (see picture on previous page). Two small wooden wedges, one under either side of the door mould, facilitate its easy removal later on.

Sand is now shovelled into the area contained within the skirt wall and shaped into a rounded dome with a slight swelling towards the back, forming a half avocado shape. The sand should rise from the inner side of the skirt and be shaped to align with the inner edge of the smaller arch of the door mould. Make sure that the sand mould is no more than 50 per cent higher than the height of the door.

The small cardboard-covered cylinder directly behind the door mould represents the position of the chimney when the dome is complete. This can be made by cutting 150 mm (6 in) from a 112–125 mm (4½–5 in) stainless flue pipe (the final chimney). Push the covered pipe a little way into the sand and form a cove of sand around the base. Firm the sand down, especially around the door mould, and trowel to a smooth finish.

Step 6: Preparing the clay mix

Natural dry clay must be broken up and passed through a strong mesh.

It is assumed you have already done some prospecting and found a suitable natural clay source (see Appendix 4: Prospecting for and testing natural clay). If no natural clay is available it may be necessary to buy some powdered clay from a mineral supplier or pottery supply shop. It may be suggested you buy fireclay powder for such a project, but experience suggests that some fireclays are so 'short' they will not give you the necessary binding strength. It is better to purchase plastic 'ball' clay or terra cotta.

The natural dry clay can be broken up with a hammer and passed through a medium mesh, such as 12 mm (1/2 in) bird wire or an old mattress base. You will require approximately 3 x 8 litre buckets (3 x US 2 gallon buckets) of sieved dry clay.

Kneading the clay mix by 'walking' on canvas.

Assuming your clay is judged to be highly plastic (i.e. easily mouldable and holds firmly together), you will need to add equal parts of sand (brickies sand, seeing it is already in use) and stone dust (crusher dust, cracker dust, quarry fines of 6 mm/¼ in minus screenings). If the clay is only partially plastic, you will need less sand and stone dust. To this combination add 10 per cent by volume ordinary Portland cement. Mix dry and set one-third aside.

Place the remaining two-thirds of the mix in a wheelbarrow or large container and, using a spade or hoe, mix with enough water to form a partially soft, sticky mass. On a strong canvas sheet, or similar non-shiny fabric, spread out most of the dry mix that was set aside.

Place the moistened, sticky mass onto the dry powder as if you were placing soft dough onto a bed of flour. You can begin mixing this by hand, but a simpler way is to 'walk' on top of the clay mix, using the canvas, tipping it over from time to time until it has been foot-kneaded into a homogeneous mix.

Note My observations suggest that many oven builders using some form of clay mix to tend to add too much clay to the mix in the belief that it is necessary for strength. On other occasions the mix is used in too wet a state. Both situations lead to excessive shrinkage and therefore cracking.

Step 7: Forming the clay mix thermal layer

After covering the sand mould with a layer of very thin plastic sheeting (painter's drop sheet is ideal) to prevent the clay mix picking up sand, make thin pancake shapes of clay mix and begin laying them over the spine of the dome and down the sides in a fish-scale overlap. This layer

Applying the clay mix to the sand mould.

Applying the clay mix to the sand mould.

should be no more than 12 mm (½ in) thick.

Tap each pancake together slightly until the whole dome surface is covered and meets the top of the paver skirt. Now the clay mix can be beaten more heavily with hands or wooden beaters to consolidate the layer.

Once the first layer is complete, cover it with subsequent layers until the clay mix is fully used. The total thermal (hot face) mass should be no less than 50 mm (2 in) thick. The clay mix may extend over the skirt wall and the buttress to the insulation level, but leave a gap of at least 20 mm (¾ in) at the three points nearest to the frame edge.

It is important that the layers of clay mix be added one after another in rapid succession. Any delay will result in different drying rates (and shrinkage) which could lead to delamination during the firing of the oven.

Particular attention should be given to pressing firmly against the door mould so that the rebate step is accurately formed. A collar of clay of at least 50 mm (2 in) needs to be built up around the temporary chimney pipe, and the top made level.

If a temperature probe is to be introduced, a sharpened, oiled piece of wooden dowel just slightly larger than the probe shaft should be pushed through the wall of the dome at about half internal dome height and a third of the distance back from the door. It will need to go through the wall at an oblique angle if it is to be read from the front of the oven.

Step 8: Removing the sand mould and drying the oven

Once the clay mix thermal layer has become firmer (this could take some hours) through air drying and setting (due to the cement addition) it is time to remove the door mould, the short pipe where the chimney will go, and the sand mould. While it does not have to be done as rapidly as during a workshop, it is important to empty the sand from the oven before the clay mix dries completely. This is because the clay mix shrinks on drying, but the sand doesn't, so serious cracking of the dome would occur.

The sand must be removed before the clay mix dries out too far.

Step 9: Covering the oven with an insulation layer

The insulation need not cover the chimney collar.

Before moving on to applying the wet insulation layer, there is some advantage in first 'firing up' the oven so that any shrinkage cracks which may have occurred on drying can be repaired. It is not uncommon to have some horizontal cracking where the dome meets the paver skirt, and some short vertical cracks usually occur rising from the same position. These are not serious structural cracks and are easily filled.

In heating the oven for the first time, it is very important to take this extremely slowly. Rapid heating will turn the moisture contained in the dome (although it may feel bone dry), to steam and the clay mix will 'blow'. The easiest way to introduce low and steady heat to the oven chamber is with a gas ring burner or similar small heater.

The heater can be slowly turned up over several hours until you are certain that no moisture remains in the dome. If you have introduced a temperature probe the interior temperature should have reached about 150° C (300° F). At this stage a small wood fire can be introduced to increase the temperature. The fire should also increase slowly until the temperature reaches about 400° C (750° F).

Wood fire heating unfinished dome.

Now that the oven dome is very hot any cracks will be at their widest, through expansion, so it is an ideal time to fill them with fluid clay 'paint' made from 3 parts sand and one part clay and a little cement. Mix the ingredients dry and add enough water to make a fluid capable of passing through a kitchen sieve.

Brush the mix fairly liberally across the cracks so that the 'paint' pours into the cracks. With the oven being hot the 'paint' will dry rapidly and with continued application the cracks will soon be filled.

Brushing clay 'paint' into cracks.

When all the cracks are filled and the oven is still hot is an ideal time to cover the dome with the insulation layer. There is some benefit in having the oven hot for this process because as the insulation mix is particularly wet the heat minimises the risk of water entering the dry clay mix and causing it to soften and possibly collapse. It is better to apply the insulation in two layers, allowing a little drying and setting in between coats.

To maximise the insulating qualities keep the binding materials, which are dense, to a minimum. Divide the contents of a full bag of vermiculite (or perlite), normally 100 litres (23 US gallons dry) into two equal amounts.

Mix up a quantity of insulation in the ratio of 10 parts vermiculite, one part sieved clay and one part cement in a barrow, then add water until a sloppy mixture is achieved. Place it over the dome of the oven in small handfuls. To retain maximum aeration and therefore insulation do not pack it down tightly.

Once the first layer of insulation mix has become firm the second layer can

be applied. As that begins to become firmer the surface can be trowelled to a smooth finish.

Applying the first layer of insulation.

Trowelling the second insulation layer smooth.

Step 10: Applying a 'paintable' finishing coat

After the insulation coat has become firm and almost dry, the whole surface can be painted with a coating of 6 parts sand, 1 part clay and 1 part cement, with the addition of colouring oxides if you wish, mixed with enough water to be able to pass through a kitchen sieve to form a creamy consistency.

Applying a finishing coat – here tinted with a mixture of cement oxides.

The finished oven.

It is worth keeping some of this final 'paint' mixture aside as a dry powder for your first serious firing. If small surface cracks should appear in the insulation coat because of further shrinkage they can be painted over and filled.

Note This low-tech oven is *not* waterproof and should be protected from rain with a roof structure, a tarpaulin or plastic sheeting – but only when it has cooled down.

I am often asked if a clay oven can be given a concrete cap to waterproof it, but a problem can arise when the hot oven expands and forces the concrete to crack.

If the oven was first covered with ceramic blanket (see Chapter 5, Building Your Oven with New Materials) and then a concrete cap, the ceramic blanket would act as a 'cushion' between the layers and cracking would be prevented. You would have to allow for the extra thicknesses in your initial planning.

Stone and rock ovens

It has long been known that some natural stone is particularly good at withstanding heat, especially talc and limestone. There are many examples, still in existence, of old limestone built ovens, especially in the south of France. Many of these are made from cut and shaped limestone.

I must admit that when I first heard of ovens being built from field rocks I could not help recalling the scouting experiences of my youth, when the combination of rocks and campfire could lead to such an explosion that life and limb could be in jeopardy. In retrospect, it was probably the fact that most of these rocks were damp and immediately subjected to intense heat that caused an explosion, rather than the mineral composition of the rocks.

When conducting a workshop in Red Deer, Canada, I was fascinated to hear from one of the participants of a number of stone-built ovens that had been built along the old Kettle Valley Railroad in British Columbia. This train line was built in the early 1900s to service the expanding mining industries and as part of the labour force many immigrant workers were employed, including Italians. It was mostly the Italian labourers who built the stone ovens at their camps for baking bread. Although the railway line has long been abandoned the ovens remain dotted at intervals along the old track.

During my visit to Canada my schedule left me no opportunity to see these ovens for myself but I did find a fascinating 1991 article by historian and archaeologist Priscilla Wegars, 'Who's been working on the railroad?', which detailed much of the history of similar ovens built along railroads in North America and included a brief but intriguing reference to similar stone ovens in Australia, thought to be 'Chinese ovens'.

Workers taking bread from a rock oven at French Gulch in Montana. The sign held by the man at second left (translated) reads 'This is our oven, March 1906'. Courtesy Maureen and Mike Mansfield Library, University of Montana.

I was sceptical, as I had never heard of any such ovens and did not think the Chinese had a tradition of baking or roasting in ovens of any sort. I was wrong. I found that throughout many Australian mining settlements (mainly gold), where large numbers of Chinese miners congregated, from the mid nineteenth century onwards, there were a number of stone ovens built for

Chinese pig oven at Twelve Mile, in the Northern Territory, Australia. Courtesy Peter Bell.

roasting whole pigs, particularly for festive occasions. These ovens were open topped so that the pigs could be lowered into the hot, deep, rock-lined pit. The opening would be covered with metal sheets and the pigs roasted for some hours. A small opening at the base of the oven allowed coals to be raked out.

My fascination with the use of local stones as oven-building material, especially by the Italians along the Kettle Valley Railroad, led me to recall that my grandparents had once lived in the small Victorian town of Hepburn Springs where, in the mid 1800s, many Italians and Italian-speaking Swiss had settled. Most had come to Australia to escape the agricultural poverty and political upheavals of the northern Italian border regions and to establish a better life in the goldfields of Victoria. I wondered if they, too, might have used the stone that was readily available in the area for ovens, as there were certainly few other materials that could have been used, apart from clay. I contacted David Endicott from the local historical society, who said he could show me a couple of sites that might be of interest.

He guided me into what were once old mining settlements around Yandoit, now returning to native bush, and there we found similar stone structures to those of Canada, undoubtedly ovens from the presence of the 'fired' clay which bonded the stones together. One site presented two ovens, side by side, next to a small creek that had powered a small mill for grinding wheat. Established by two Italian brothers around the 1860s, this was formerly a bakery which supplied the local mining area with bread. Occasional flooding of the creek over the past 150 years had taken its toll and the fronts of the ovens had been washed away.

The rocks used, according to my geologist neighbour, were quartzitic sandstone and vesicular basalt (a honeycombed lava). With my background in ceramics I would have been suspicious of using quartz (silica)-based rock because if silica is heated to 573° C (1063° F), which is well within the possibility of a wood-fired oven, the silica goes through a sudden expansion and also a contraction when cooled below that temperature. This can lead to cracking. I did notice, however, that the stones in the old bakery ovens were placed on edge to form an arched roof, so they would not have suffered from delamination as so often happens if a face is exposed to heat, suggesting that its builders had been aware of the risk.

The ruins of the old stone-built ovens of the Yandoit Bakery.

I have not had personal experience in using natural rock or stones, but for the wood-fired enthusiast who is at a great distance from any conventional oven-building materials, and has a ready source of stone available, it may be an alternative way to build an oven. It would probably be advisable to make some tests before committing to a major undertaking.

A ready-made oven (well, almost)

In many parts of the world termites are common, particularly in Australia, and some termite mounds resemble closely the shape of a domed oven. It is know that some of the early settlers in Australia would burn out the fibrous interior of these mounds, cut an entrance in the side of the thick wall, heat it up with wood and bake bread in the cleaned-out interior using the remaining residual heat. The Dutch pioneers in South Africa were also known to have used termite mounds for the same thing.

Many years ago, during a kiln camp on my coastal property, some of my students decided to try an abandoned termite mound as a pottery kiln. They first cut a hole to the fibrous interior at the base of the mound and made a hole at the top. After establishing a smouldering fire in the fibrous material at the base they left the fire to its own devices overnight and by morning the whole interior had been emptied, leaving only the thick outer shell, varying in thickness from 100–150 mm (4–6 in).

After building a barrel arch firebox leading into the mound at the base, and cutting a doorway a third of the way up to place some kiln shelving to support their pottery, they established a small fire and gradually began to heat up the 'termite kiln'. After about ten hours of steady rising heat from the wood-burning firebox the temperature rose to 850° C (1562° F) without causing any cracking to the mound. Such firings were repeated many times before the

weather eventually took its toll.

The clay 'mix' used by the termites in the outer shell of their mounds is near perfect for building a low-tech oven. It contains a balanced mix of clay and sand, already naturally 'graded' as they bring each particle from below ground in their mandibles. You do not see cracking occurring in termite mounds because of shrinkage.

Termite mound in natural surroundings.

Alan Gray, editor of *Earth Garden* magazine, was keen to build a low-tech oven at his home in Broome, in remote north-western Australia. As Broome is thousands of kilometres from the nearest centre where refractory materials were available, and the humble housebrick was a rare commodity, he decided to build his oven from reconstituted termite mound. Following the construction method of building a low-tech oven, learned at a workshop he had previously attended, Alan constructed a very efficient oven that continues to give satisfactory results and pleasure to this day.

I'm not advocating that you break up viable termite mounds to get a ready-to-go low-tech oven clay mixture, but termites do eventually exhaust their food supply and move on, so look for abandoned mounds.

5   Building an Oven from Brick

Using fired clay bricks for the construction of a wood-fired oven has a history of thousands of years, as evidenced by the large number of brick ovens found in the 2000-year-old city of Pompeii.

There is a widely held belief that when it comes to building a wood-fired oven you must use firebricks. This is not so. Firebricks, because of their high alumina content, are capable of withstanding very high temperatures of 1200° C (2192° F) and above. They are particularly suited to kilns and furnaces but are an excessive expense when it comes to the temperatures to which most wood-fired ovens are subjected.

In the case of a commercial wood-fired oven that is constantly in use I would recommend firebricks, but for the intermittent use that a home wood-fired oven gets, modern, solid, pressed housebricks are satisfactory. Most modern bricks and clay pavers are fired at temperatures around 1100° C (2012° F), which is well above any temperature likely to be experienced in a wood-fired oven, even under the coals of the fire. If there is a choice, select lighter coloured bricks as they generally have a higher alumina content.

During discussion sessions at workshops I have often been asked 'Don't firebricks hold the heat better?' The answer lies in the density of the brick; while most firebricks are denser than common bricks the difference is minimal and would have little impact on the cooking outcome. It is true that there is slightly less expansion/contraction in a firebrick but, again, the difference is so small that it should not be of concern.

Another common question relates to the suitability of using soft-fired, hand-made bricks in a wood-fired oven. As these bricks are less compact, or bonded, in structure than bricks fired at higher temperatures they are more easily worn by abrasive action so I would not use them on the floor or lower walls of the oven, but they will certainly stand the temperatures. My own home fireplace is built from bricks fired, on site, when the house was built in 1881, and they are certainly 'soft'. Despite being subjected to huge log fires for the last 130 years they are still sound, with only the lime mortar bonding them together receding a little.

To most amateur builders and handypersons the thought of tackling a brick dome for an oven is too daunting; they assume you need the architectural expertise of a Michelangelo and the bricklaying skills of a professional. This following section should be able to convince the reader that it is not that mysterious, nor difficult. I've had a number of former workshop participants go on to build their own brick ovens without ever having laid a brick in their lives before.

Step 1: Building a base

Base made of masonry blocks.

There are a number of options for building a base, as outlined in the previous chapter, but for a brick oven, because of the thick thermal mass in the dome, which retains a steady heat for a lengthy period, it would seem appropriate to place it on a base that would also retain heat for a considerable time. A brick oven is particularly suited to long, slow cooking of roasts and to multiple bread baking periods. That is not to suggest that it would not be suitable for pizzas – but the oven will take more time, and fuel, to heat up.

The base in this case is built of masonry blocks and is 1000 mm (39 in) high and 1600 mm (5 ft 3 in) square, large enough to allow for a tiled surround, especially in front of the oven. The base allows for a 'heat bank' below the floor of the oven so a false floor of 12 mm (½ in) compressed cement sheeting, sitting on 4 x 50 mm (2 in) angle iron supports, is incorporated at the second last course of blocks, 200 mm (8 in) below the oven floor level.

The top course of channel blocks is reinforced with 12 mm (1/2 in) rod and the central cavity on three sides is core filled with concrete to the 100 mm (4 in) reinforced concrete foundation slab below. The remainder of the cavities is filled only to the depth of the last course.

Step 2: Insulating the 'heat bank'

The 'heat bank' well is lined with insulation, in this case insulating bricks, but it

Insulating bricks line the 'heat bank' well.

could have been CalSil board, AAC (Hebel block) or a poured vermiculite/concrete layer.

If an ash dump slot is desired it should be incorporated at this point (at the oven door mouth) but it will eliminate the possibility of using the space beneath as wood storage. The ash dump will require a concrete or brick entry to the void below the oven.

Step 3: Filling the 'heat bank'

The remaining 112 mm (4½ in) depth of the well is now filled with moist decomposed granite (granitic sand, fine gravel). Thin layers are shovelled in and packed down firmly to consolidate the granite. This process is continued until it reaches the top of the block work, and made level.

Filling the 'heat bank' with moist decomposed granite.

Step 4: Forming a bed for the oven floor

Add a thin layer of brickies sand over the decomposed granite to form a

Screeding the thin layer of brickies sand.

bed for the oven floor. With 10 mm (3/8 in) wooden runners along two sides of the blocks, level the sand with a screed.

Guide lines are marked in the levelled sand.

Step 5: Laying the floor

Mark a front line in the sand bed to indicate where the outside tiles will be laid, and a central line the length of the base. You are now ready to lay the oven floor.

Oven floor of 50 mm (2 in) thick ceramic pavers is laid.

The floor in this case is made from 50 mm (2 in) thick ceramic pavers, but larger firebrick tiles could have been used. The pavers are firmly tapped into place with a rubber mallet until the floor is perfectly flat. No bonding mortar is used.

Step 6: Establishing a perimeter wall

A perimeter wall of bricks laid in a 'soldier' pattern establishes the dimensions of the inside of the oven. As the full length of the brick is considered too high, each brick was cut at an angle about two-thirds its length

Bricks cut at an angle and re-joined to create an arch springer.

and the off-cut reversed and bonded back to the other part of the brick, using air-set mortar, to act as an arch 'springer'. Depending on what profile you wish the dome to take, the angle you cut the 'soldier' bricks is likely to be anywhere between 15 and 22 degrees from the horizontal, to form a dome with a lower profile than a semi-circle. This can first be established on paper.

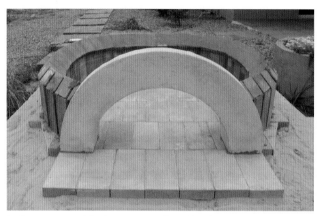

Refractory castable door stop arch set in place.

The refractory castable 'door stop' arch (see Appendix 2: Making arches and door entries) is set into place using air-set mortar, and the course of 'soldier/ springer' bricks is also bonded into place following an oval pencil line marked on the floor tiles. The arch could have been made using bricks over conventional formwork.

Step 7: Buttressing the perimeter wall

A buttress is added to support the perimeter wall.

The short vertical wall of perimeter bricks is now given support with a buttress of refractory castable or Portland cement-based concrete (see Chapter 4, step 4 for details).

Step 8: Beginning the oven dome

Half bricks positioned against a plywood profile establish the curve of the lower section of the dome. The first few courses can be laid without support, giving an opportunity to fill any gaps on the inside of the dome as well as allowing you to clean the surface of excess mortar.

The inside edges of the bricks almost touch other while the wider gaps on the

outside are held in position with stiffer mortar. Small pieces of broken brick can be wedged into the wider gaps if there is a tendency for the bricks to slump downwards. The mortar used in this case was a powdered commercial mortar mixed with 20 per cent fireclay for extra plasticity. (See Glossary for more information on alternative mortars.)

Half bricks are used for the first course of the dome.

Step 9: Completing the oven dome

A sand mould makes the task of completing the dome much simpler. Note the end of a round dowel marking the desired height of the centre of the dome.

The half bricks can be built up, without support, until the point where gravity takes over and they tend to fall inwards. If the dome is being constructed using tapered bricks and the joints are very thin then it is possible to complete the whole dome without support.

In this case there is need for support and the easiest way, especially as the dome is slightly oval, is to use a sand mould. If the dome is very large or there is a shortage of sand, an elevated platform of thin plywood or particle board (in two pieces, if you wish to retrieve it through the door opening) is built on a brick piers to the level of the last course of bricks laid. If there is plenty of sand the whole oven can be filled.

Shape the sand to a continuation of the curve of the dome and cover it in a thin sheet of plastic.

Completing the bricklaying.

The remaining courses can now continue with the inner faces of the bricks resting against the shape formed by the sand mould. As each course has a successively smaller radius it becomes necessary to use one-third bricks and eventually quarter-bricks if you prefer not to have great gaps at the top of the dome.

As the top of the dome becomes more level the bricks will sit on the sand mould without needing to be held in position with mortar. They can be partially bonded and the gaps can be filled by pouring a fluid refractory castable or mortar over the top of the bricks.

A coat of castable fills any gaps between the bricks and holds everything together.

The completed dome can be given a coat of castable to seal everything together and to fill any remaining gaps. If a temperature probe is to be incorporated an appropriate hole can be drilled at this stage, using a masonry bit. Ceramic tubes that make the insertion and withdrawal of the probe much easier are available.

Step 11: Insulating the dome

The dome can now be covered with insulation. If you are using ceramic fibre it is essential to protect yourself from the fine particles that may be shed during instalment. One roll of ceramic blanket will enable you to cover much of the dome in a double layer if the oven is of modest size.

Wear protection against the fine particles that come from ceramic fibre material.

With the ceramic blanket in place the dome is now ready to be covered with a protective cap of concrete. Unless you are skilled at cutting tiles on a curve it is easier to bring the concrete cap over the tiles laid on the shelf around the base of the oven. The tiles have been laid with a large gap between dome and tiles to avoid any lateral pressure being exerted by the expanding oven. The gap can be filled with vermiculite or ceramic blanket to prevent it being filled with concrete.

Ready for applying the concrete cap over the ceramic blanket.

Step 12: The protective cap

As the blanket will prevent excessive heat passing through to the protective cap there is no need to use high-temperature materials for the cap. Apply the concrete cap directly over the ceramic blanket. It should be at least 25 mm (1 in) thick. A standard concrete is used – 3 parts fine crushed stone, 2 parts sand, 1 part cement.

You will note from the previous picture that the outer cast arch which contains the outlet hole for escaping gases has been installed, and above that the manifold or transition box that transfers a rectangular opening to a circular opening ready to take the stainless steel flue pipe. Both these sections could be formed in brick. The gases then pass through the tapered transition box to the round 150 mm (6 in) stainless steel flue pipe. For the casting of these two sections

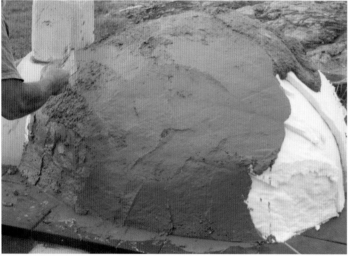

Applying the concrete cap over the ceramic blanket.

see Appendixes 2 and 3.

The use of refractory castable or brick is preferable to mild steel components in this area as the alkaline nature of wood smoke and ash, especially if it is moist during the early light-up stage can quickly cause deterioration of the steel. Stainless steel would be a far better choice

Step 13: The outer arch for an external flue

The outer arch, showing the recessed channel which encourages the exiting gases to be delivered to the rectangular opening above the doorway.

Step 14: The completed oven

The final render coat and grouting of the surrounding tiles was purposely not completed before the first firing of the oven in case there was some movement, through expansion, causing slight cracking and movement of tiles. There wasn't.

The near-completed oven after its first firing. A final brushed render coat with coloured oxide and waterproofing additive can now be applied. The surrounding tiles can also be grouted.

6   Building an Oven from New Materials

The common clay brick and resources from Mother Earth have served oven builders for millennia, but their quality and reliability has been as varied as the places in which they were produced. The term 'new materials' covers a broad range of refractory materials that have been developed during the modern industrial age and in more recent times, largely for the kiln and furnace industries, as demand for greater quality and less costly products increased. Many have now been employed by oven builders because of their efficiency, longevity and quality.

The main items that the amateur wood-fired oven builder is likely to use are firebricks, insulation bricks and boards, high alumina cements and castables (high temperature concrete), ceramic blanket (discovered in 1942 but developed by NASA for making insulating tiles for rockets re-entering Earth's atmosphere) and stainless steel 'needles' for reinforcing castables.

In the following description of building a high-tech oven you will see many of the above products being used. This oven plan is based on an oval with the dome of the oven sitting on the firebrick hearth tiles. The base measures 1200 x 1500 mm (42 x 59 in) with provision for a tiled ledge in front of the oven. The internal dimensions will be approximately 900 x 1050 mm (35 x 41 in) but can be made to a much larger size.

Step 1: Laying the hearth tiles on the base

After creating a smooth sand bed

Laying the hearth tiles on a sand base similar to that described in Chapter 5, 'Building a brick oven'. The tiles could also have been laid on insulating bricks to conserve more heat as an alternative under-floor system to the 'heat bank'.

over the 'heat bank', the front edge and central lines are marked out ready for placing the oven hearth tiles. In this case 300 x 300 x 40 mm (12 x 12 x 1¾ in) fire brick tiles are used.

The tiles need to be carefully placed onto the sand bed directly from above. Sliding them into position will form a wave of sand in front of the tile and produce a gap between tiles. There is no need for bonding materials.

Shape some of the hearth tiles to form the oval shape (use a diamond-tipped cutting disc or masonry disc on a hand-grinder if you don't have a brick saw), and tap all the tiles firmly into the sand bed to form an even surface.

Step 2: Placing the front arch for the door

Two pre-cast arches are now bonded together with air-set mortar to form a rebated door opening (see Appendix 2: Making arches and door entries).

A more complicated mould could have created the same form as one piece but the weight would have been too much to handle.

Pre-cast door arches bonded together are placed in position.

Step 3: Laying a vertical perimeter 'skirt' wall

A paver perimeter 'skirt' similar to that described for the low-tech clay oven is incorporated in this construction, although you could build a thicker skirt with bricks in a 'soldier' pattern. As this oven is to have an internal chimney the

The first brick of the perimeter 'skirt' is cut to fit against the door arch.

skirt can be set back 25 mm (1 in) from the arch inner edge. Cut the first paver to fit to the arch and bond the perimeter of pavers to the floor, and to each other, with air-set mortar (as described in Chapter 4).

Step 4: Buttressing the skirt wall

Applying the buttressing mix.

After the perimeter wall has been bonded to the floor fill any gaps with air-set mortar and clean all surfaces. The perimeter wall can be buttressed with either a high-temperature cement mix or a Portland cement mix (see Chapter 4 for details). As the buttress serves no structural function when the dome is complete, there is no real necessity to use high-temperature materials. The thermal mass qualities of either mixture will remain the most important benefit once the dome is complete and the oven is being used.

When applying the buttress material, keep it at least 50 mm (2 in) in from the edge of the base to allow for the thickness of the insulation blanket and concrete protective cap.

Step 5: Forming the sand mould

The finished sand mould.

As with the low-tech clay oven, the sand mould should be shaped within the perimeter skirt and to within 25 mm (1 in) of the inner arch edge. A temporary flue pipe with cardboard sleeve is placed centrally, directly behind the arch. The sand should be built up at the base of this pipe to encourage the smoke and hot gases to enter the flue rather than emerge through the doorway.

For this size oven the flue pipe should be no less than 140 mm (5½ in) in diameter.

Step 6: Mixing the castable

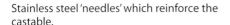

Stainless steel 'needles' which reinforce the castable.

Mixing the castable.

In order to have a bubble-free, smooth inner surface to the cast dome it is best to apply the castable in thin layers (especially the first) to eventually to build up the dome to, at least, 50 mm (2 in) thick.

Castable, capable of withstanding a temperature of 1200° C (2192° F), normally comes as a pre-mixed dry powder and simply requires the addition of water. It comprises a mixture of high-alumina, high-temperature cement and a combination of high-alumina, calcined (fired) aggregates. Some castables have the addition of fine synthetic fibres to hold the material together while it is being worked, but these burn out when heated.

The addition of 'needles' (of stainless steel) creates an interlocking matrix thus ensuring the dome will be well reinforced and resistant to cracking. These needles are capable of withstanding high temperatures and will not rust or decay. It is recommended that they be mixed with the castable at the rate of 2 per cent, by weight – that is, about a very large handful per 25 kilo (55 lb) bag of castable.

For an oven this size you will require approximately two bags of castable for the arches and flue pipe base, plus six bags to cover the dome.

Mix the needles with the castable dry and then add water until a thick porridge consistency is achieved. The initial layer needs to be soft enough to press tightly to the plastic-covered surface but not so fluid that it will run off the plastic membrane protecting the sand mould.

Step 7: Applying the castable

In building up the layers of castable establish a level platform beneath the damper.

Once the sand mould has been covered with a very thin plastic membrane (to stop sand adhering to the castable), the mixture can be shovelled to the top of the dome and 'puddled', by tapping the mixture gently with your hands, spreading it slowly over and down to the top of the perimeter skirt.

Castable tends to set more quickly than Portland cement concrete, so within an hour or so it will be firm enough to apply subsequent layers. You do not need to immediately add succeeding layers, as for a clay-based oven, as very little shrinkage takes place when castable sets.

The second and following layers can be made slightly thicker and needles can also be added for extra strength. Gradually build up a horizontal platform around the temporary flue pipe to take the damper and flue base as described in Appendix 3: Dampers and chimney bases.

Three or four layers should be sufficient to bring the thickness to at least 50 mm (2 in).

Positioning the sliding damper and removing the temporary short flue sleeve.

Step 8: Positioning the damper

Once the castable 'platform' around the temporary chimney is level, the sliding ceramic damper can be positioned. This is usually just above the door arch with the mouth of the damper level with where you would like to bring the outer layer of the dome. The damper is constructed from thin kiln shelving, available at refractory suppliers or pottery stores. It has been pre-made and glued together with epoxy. (see Appendix 3: Dampers and chimney bases.)

Castable can be brought up level with the top edge of the damper to hold it in position. The short metal pipe (a piece cut from the length of chosen flue pipe) can now be removed along with the cardboard liner.

Securing the cast flue pipe base with castable.

Step 9: Positioning the flue pipe base

The cast flue pipe base (see Appendix 3: Dampers and chimney bases) is positioned on top of the damper to be directly in line with the hole beneath it and secured in position with some castable. To prevent the castable fouling the ceramic slide of the damper, fill in any gaps with paper or sand.

Step 10: Covering the dome with ceramic blanket

Ceramic blanket covering the dome.

The oven dome can now be covered with ceramic blanket as for the brick oven. Keep the blanket back at least 50 mm (2 in) from where you would like the concrete cover to finish (either midway on the arch or to the very edge of the arch.

Remember to use protective gear.

Step 11: Applying the concrete protective 'cap'

Drilling a hole in the concrete cap to take a ceramic sheath to hold a temperature probe

Again, following the same procedure as for the brick oven, the ceramic blanket can be covered with a protective concrete cap. This covering is a standard Portland cement concrete of 3 parts fine crushed stone (as aggregate), 2 parts sand and 1 part cement.

If a temperature probe is to be incorporated, a ceramic sheath can be inserted at this stage as long as the castable has not set fully hard. The probe sheath can be more easily inserted when the castable is being applied, but will need to be held in place until the castable sets.

Step 12: Applying a render coat

Applying a coloured render coat.

Once the concrete cap is set you can be sure that the castable layer has also set, so the sand mould can be removed through the doorway.

As this particular oven was being built during a workshop, the render coat was applied before firing the oven for the first time. Delaying the render coat until after the first firing allows movement to take place so that any minor cracking revealed can be repaired before being covered by the final coat.

The render mix is 4½ parts sand (brickies or rendering), 1 part cement and ½ part hydrated lime, plus any colouring oxide and cement-compatible waterproof additive.

Step 13: The job completed

When the project is complete you should wait a few more days to allow all layers to cure and dry out before bringing the oven very slowly up to cooking temperatures – there's a lot of water in there to dry out.

A little more render over the oven base and the project will be complete.

7 Recipes: Exploring the Oven's Diverse Uses

At times, when I have been introduced to someone and they learn that I have some connection with wood-fired ovens their questions often seem to centre around cooking pizza. When I point out that a wood-fired oven has a greater diversity of uses than simply cooking pizza, and mention some of the other dishes that can be cooked in such an oven the response is usually, 'Really? You can cook that in a wood-fired oven as well?'

So to reinforce the truth that a wood-fired oven is not simply a specialist item for cooking pizza, I have gathered a few recipes from friends and former past workshop participants, who have either built their own oven, have hosted a workshop or have one that I've built for them – with one exception, which will be obvious.

This collection does not include all the types of dishes that can be cooked in a wood-fired oven, but should give you some indication of its diversity of use.

Pizza

I have so many photos of pizzas, and so many recipes, that I thought a generic photo would suffice as an example. Any hunt for a book on pizzas or an internet search for a recipe will have you swamped with choice.

Although the modern pizza originated in Naples, and it is still thought of as typically Italian, it has become so widespread as to be considered an international favourite. Each country seems to have given the pizza a local touch, with many styles so removed from the classic range it must make the Italians squirm.

I remember a time, well before I was involved in making wood-fired ovens, when I was visiting my daughter, then on student exchange in Milan, and she ordered my favourite pizza, marinara. When it arrived at our table I thought her newly acquired ability to speak Italian was well short of being competent. 'Kirsty!' I exclaimed, 'I ordered marinara', as I looked down at the very thin

Cooking pizzas in a low-tech oven on the second day of a workshop.

baked dough with a mere smear of tomato paste on top. 'Dad, that *is* marinara!' I had become so used to the Melbourne version – a thicker dough piled high with prawns, mussels, baby octopus and clams – that I imagined I had been cheated.

Since that time I have become more appreciative of thin crust and limited toppings and believe the term 'less is more' aptly applies to pizza making.

Breads

If pizzas are so strongly associated with wood-fired ovens in the modern age then it is bread that is synonymous with the historical past of such ovens. Every culture seems to have a distinctive bread style, from flat unleavened breads, whose history goes back to ancient times, through to the round, plump, yeast-inflated breads of the modern age.

There is no point in attempting to offer more than just a few bread recipes, for there are dozens of books on the subject and nearly all wood-fired oven

Bread can be baked in a container or as simple cobs.

A well-baked sourdough loaf straight from the oven.

An olive bread baked during a workshop.

Hot bread emerging from a workshop
low-tech oven.

owners eventually try their hand at baking some form of bread that appeals, be it sourdough rye, ciabatta or the hundreds of styles in between.

Many wood-fired oven builders and owners become passionate about the artisan style bread that such ovens produce and have written knowledgeable books on the subject, none better than Daniel Wing and Alan Scott in *The Bread Builders*. This book is not a collection of recipes but a thorough explanation of the physiology of dough development and the process of baking that suits the particular nature of wood-fired oven baking.

Harry's naan bread

Harry's naan bread.

Recently, I made a tandoori oven for my friends and neighbours, Rachel and Phil, and while we have had great success with tandoori chicken on skewers we have had no end of trouble in getting the naan bread to stick to the walls of the oven. We have been blaming our failures on the type of flour used, the consistency of the dough mix, even the fact that the oven was new and not 'broken in', but I suspect it is a tricky business and we have not developed the skills required to successfully attach the bread to the vertical walls of the tandoor.

I think Harry has got the game sewn up – why fight gravity when the hot floor of the wood-fired oven will do just as well? The hot coals at the back of the oven can produce the typical scorched surface of the naan bread and I'm sure if you hooked it out of the oven it would produce the pulled stretch look of a true naan. It may not be authentic but it is better than seeing your dough peel off the walls of the tandoor and fall into the fire below. Harry has become something of an expert in producing numerous dishes from the clay-based low-tech oven and with his family has gone on to build another larger oven, made largely from reconstituted termite mound.

There are numerous recipes for naan bread but you may like to try this one.

1½ teaspoons dry yeast   1 teaspoon salt (or to taste)
1 cup warm water   6 tablespoons ghee (clarified butter)
1½ teaspoons sugar   3 tablespoons yoghurt
3 cups plain (all-purpose) flour

Add the dry yeast and sugar to the warm water and stir till the yeast is dissolved. Cover and leave aside for 10 minutes or until the mixture begins to froth. This indicates the yeast is active. Keep aside.

Mix the flour and salt and sift through a very fine sieve. Put it into a large mixing bowl and now add the yeast mixture, 3 tablespoons of ghee and all the yoghurt. Use your fingertips to mix all this into a soft dough. Once mixed, flour a clean, flat surface (like your kitchen counter) and knead the dough till it is smooth and stretchy (elastic).

Grease a large bowl with a few drops of cooking oil and put the dough in it. Cover and allow to rest for about 90 minutes or till the dough doubles in volume. Now punch the dough down and knead again for 10 minutes. Divide into 8 sections and roll into balls between your palms.

Lightly flour the surface on which you kneaded the dough and roll out each ball until you have a circle 18–20 cm (7–8 in) in diameter and about 12 mm (1/2 in) thick. You can pat them into circles with your hands if you prefer.

Place on the floor of the oven at about 200° C (400° F) until judged to be cooked.

Remove the breads from oven and brush with ghee and a little crushed garlic if you wish.

Uzbek bread

When Anna, who lived in Uzbekistan for much of her youth, told me of this method of baking

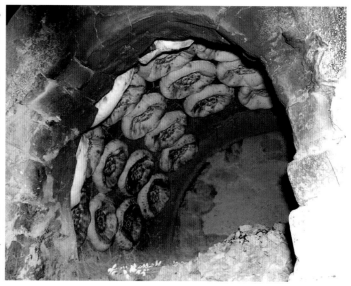

bread I was somewhat incredulous. If it's difficult to get naan to adhere to a vertical surface, how on earth do they get their puffy round breads to stick overhead?

If you would like to see a fascinating video of the process do an internet search of 'youtube uzbek bread'. If you're game enough to try – good luck!

Seafood

Ray's crayfish tails

A feast fit for the gods.

Now, crayfish is my dream food, and at the price you now have to pay for it these days, it is becoming a distant dream. Ray, my long-time old school friend, built his wood-fired oven in a coastal suburb of Perth, Western Australia, where the crayfish abound. With boat and private licence he regularly catches crayfish (the Australian version of lobster) not far from his home. If you're lucky enough to get your hands on such a delicacy you might like to try Ray's method of cooking it.

This dish requires a Scanpan or other heavy cast-iron oven pan that retains an even heat.

Cut the crayfish tails longitudinally and devein the half that requires it. Lay the tails, shell side down, in the lightly oiled pan and pour over a small jug full of garlic butter.

Place in the oven at a temperature of about 200–250° C (400–475° F), turning the pan occasionally to make sure cooking is even. When the flesh changes colour from opaque to white (4-5 minutes), remove the pan and turn the tails over so they are flesh side down.

Return the pan to the oven and cook for only another 2–3 minutes. Avoid overcooking as the flesh will dry out.

The crayfish can be served as is or with your favourite sauce.

Rick's smoked fish

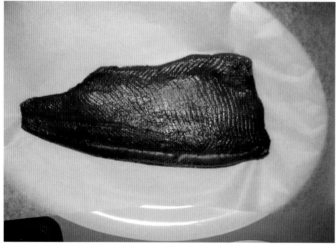
A smoked fish fillet.

Rick has made something of a specialty in smoking food in his wood-fired oven. Fish is one of his favourites – trout, salmon, or just about any other kind.

250 g (8 oz) coarse salt
1 cup caster sugar
1 bunch parsley
1 trout or salmon fillet around 1.5 kg (3.3 lb), skin on

Mix salt, sugar and finely chopped parsley in a bowl. Lay the fillet skin side down on a large platter, coat the flesh area with the parsley mix, cover with a cloth and refrigerate for no more than 12 hours.

Wash off the parsley mixture with cold water and pat dry with paper towel. Place the fillet skin side down on a rack sitting over a drip tray (this allows the smoke to get to the entire fillet) and place in the prepared oven for 30 to 45 minutes.

When the smoking is done, using greaseproof (wax) paper, completely wrap the fillet and leave it in the refrigerator for 24 hours. This greatly improves the flavour.

Your main aim in smoking food is to have the oven as cool as possible. Make a small fire, enough to create some coals but not to heat the oven much. It will be a battle to keep the temperature under 100° C (200° F). You also need either wood chips soaked in water for some time or stone-fruit wood, which is best used green, and produces lots of smoke along with flavour. Add a handful of chips at a time to the coals, making sure there are no flames, until the smoke slows down. Add another handful if needed. You need to be able to shut your oven down completely, that is, door shut and damper (if it has one) closed.

Remember: *Never* use treated or cured wood for any cooking.

Meat and poultry

Andrew's pork spare ribs

Andrew and his family hold an annual 'Spare Rib' cooking contest during the summer, when they are joined by other members of their family for holiday. It is a blind tasting, adjudicated by outsiders – and something I look forward to every year.

Here is Andrew's recipe for 4, which always seems to score high points.

Pork spare ribs.

2 kg (4.4 lb) pork spare ribs
1 large onion, chopped
1 tablespoon butter
4 tablespoons tomato sauce
  (ketchup)
4 tablespoons brown sugar
½ cup white vinegar

1 clove garlic, crushed
dash of Worcestershire sauce
2 teaspoons prepared mustard
3 tablespoons honey or jam
  (jelly)
dash Tabasco sauce
freshly ground black pepper

Boil spare ribs in salted water for 10 minutes until tender.

Meanwhile, brown the chopped onion in the butter, add the other ingredients and simmer until onion is tender.

Cool the meat, trim and cut into rib pieces. Place in a pan, cover with the sauce and bake for 45 minutes at 180° C (350° F).

Gerald's mixed roast (*Arrosto misto*)

Rabbit, duck, chicken and vegetables roasted to a turn.

Gerald, a former workshop participant, was able to build his oven in time for Christmas, and with great courage decided to tackle a fairly complicated dish for Christmas dinner.

He followed the recipe and instructions from Jamie Oliver's book *Jamie's Italy*. If it was as successful as the photo suggests, I think his risk-taking was well worth it.

As the recipe is fairly complex, Gerald advises referring to Jamie's book or downloading it from the internet.

Nelleke's Peking duck

Golden-skinned Peking duck.

Nelleke, a neighbour, is known locally as a 'foodie', and a very good one. Her past experiences and reputation are based on conventional oven cooking, but since acquiring a wood-fired oven (see the last photo in Chapter 1, A Brief History of Wood-fired Ovens'), she has successfully converted many of her dishes to wood-fired cooking.

The following recipe is not one you can whip up instantly, however; it requires a good deal of attention during the cooking process. If you are prepared to put the time and effort into trying this classic Chinese dish I'm sure you will be well rewarded.

1 x 3 kg (6.6 lb) duck, preferably
   with a long neck
1.5 litres (3.2 US pints) water

3 tablespoons honey
4 slices fresh ginger
2 spring onions (scallions)

Wash the duck under cold water, pat dry inside and out with kitchen paper. Tie the neck with a long length of kitchen string so that you can suspend the bird in a cool airy place for three hours or with a fan trained on it for about two hours in order to dry out the skin. (If the neck has been removed, tie the string around and under the wings.)

In a large pot, combine the water, honey, ginger and spring onions (cut in three). Bring to the boil and then, holding the string in one hand and a large spoon in the other, turn the duck from side to side until all its skin is moistened with the boiling liquid. Remove the duck from the pot and hang it up again, placing a bowl underneath it to catch any drips. Dry for another hour with a fan trained on it or up to 3 hours without the fan.

The oven should be preheated so that the whole oven is very hot – take it up to 500° C (950° F) and then down to 200° C (400° F) as the duck must go into a hot oven for the first hour and needs a total of approximately 2 hours cooking.

Untie the duck and place duck, breast side up, on a rack and set it in a roasting tin just large enough to hold it. Pour an inch of water into the tin and roast the duck in the middle of the oven for about one hour. Leave the coals burning and try and hold the oven at that temperature with the door partially closed. Take the duck out and turn it over, the return it to the oven, this time letting the temperature go down a bit. Roast for half an hour, remove and turn breast side up.

Add more wood to the still burning coals to raise the temperature again to 200° C (400° F). Return duck to the oven for a final burst of heat and roast for a further half hour.

Transfer to a cutting board and let rest.

To serve: Remove crispy skin and slice meat from carcass into pieces small enough to serve with *Po-ping* (mandarin pancakes), onion brushes and sauce.

For the sauce, place 3 tablespoons hoisin sauce, 3 teaspoons water, 1 teaspoon sesame oil and 1½ teaspoons sugar in a small pan, stirring until the sugar dissolves. Bring to boil, reduce heat and simmer uncovered for 3 minutes. Pour into small bowl and cool.

For the onion brushes, cut 12 shallots (spring onions) into 8 cm (3 in) lengths and trim roots. Make four intersecting cuts 2.5 cm (1 in) deep into each end. Place in iced water and refrigerate until cut parts curl into brush-like fans.

Bill's wild rabbit casserole

1 young rabbit cut into pieces	3 strips bacon, cut into pieces
3 tablsepoons plain flour	200 g (7 oz) pitted prunes
40 g (1½ oz) butter	1½ cups beef stock
½ cup red wine	salt and pepper

Soak prunes in water overnight.

Wild rabbit casserole and Moroccan lamb tagine

Coat rabbit pieces in flour and brown in a frying pan in melted butter.

Add all ingredients, except prunes, to casserole and place in oven at 160° C (320° F) for 30 minutes. Add drained prunes and simmer until rabbit is tender.

Serve with green vegetables and potato.

Phil's Moroccan lamb tagine

1 teaspoon turmeric
1 teaspoon paprika
¼ teaspoon cayenne pepper
1 tablespoon plain flour
300 g (10 oz) diced lamb shoulder
1 chopped onion
2 chopped garlic cloves
1 teaspoon cinnamon

1 tablespoon grated ginger
1 tablespoon tomato puree
1 teaspoon crushed coriander seeds
2/3 tin crushed tomatoes
8 dried apricots
1 tablespoon raisins or sultanas
olive oil
salt and pepper

Have oven about 160° C (320° F).

Mix turmeric, paprika, cayenne pepper and flour in a bowl. Coat lamb pieces in this mix and then place in oiled frying pan and brown. Set aside.

Fry onion and garlic with the cinnamon for a couple of minutes, then add the rest of the ingredients plus the lamb and cook until nice and hot.

Transfer to a tagine and pour in boiling water to cover ingredients. Add salt and pepper.

Place in the oven for 2 hours. It may require stirring after 1 hour.

Serve with couscous, fresh coriander and some preserved lemon.

Sweet treats

Di's summer fruit flan

A delicious mix of stone fruits and berries.

This dish is very easy and makes a great finale to a pizza session.

You can use ready-made pastry sheets or even pizza dough. Place dough on pizza tray and cover with a mixture of chopped summer fruits – peaches, plums, nectarines and berries (strawberries, raspberries, blueberries, etc). Cover liberally with brown sugar and place in 200° C (400° F) oven until the sugar caramelises.

Serve with whipped cream or ice cream.

Petronella's apple pastry

For Petronella this unconventional method of cooking fine pastries works very well.

Petronella is a trained pastry chef and during her professional career became used to the accurate controls of gas or electricity ovens. However, she has adapted wonderfully to the vagaries of the wood-fired oven and produces fine pastries of many varieties.

The photograph shows an apple pastry made with a cream cheese pastry crust and brandied apple filling that was cooked after a pizza session with the dying coals remaining in the oven.

The pastry was placed on a pizza tray lined with baking paper (parchment) and cooked in a 200° C (400° F) oven for about 30 minutes, being turned every 10 minutes or so until it was a nice brown colour all over. The door was partially closed to retain the heat.

Annette's meringues

Annette has made meringues on many occasions, taking advantage of the still warm oven the morning after an evening cooking session. She uses this age-old recipe.

4 egg whites   1 teaspoon vanilla
2¼ cups icing (confectioner's) sugar   handful of almond flakes

Whisk the egg whites with an electric mixer until foamy. Then add the sugar, about half a tablespoon at a time, while continuing to beat at a medium speed. When the mixture forms stiff peaks and is shiny, spoon large mounds (about half a cup) of the mixture onto a greased tray (or line the tray with oiled baking paper). Sprinkle the meringues with a few flaked almonds and put in oven, checking them every 20 minutes or so. They can take about an hour to cook – they just need to dry out slowly. Tap them – they should sound hollow – or test by eating one.

8   *The Wood-fired Oven Workshops*

Throughout this book I have made reference to the wood-fired oven workshops, and many of the photos of the construction processes have come from such workshops held, mainly, throughout Australia. It was largely the numerous requests for information from people in remote areas who were unable to attend a workshop that gave rise to this book, so some further explanation is warranted.

As mentioned in the introduction, it was not with any intention or plan that I began a round of regular workshops. After 40 years of academic life I was not desperate to return to teaching commitments. However, the early experiences were so enjoyable, in the company of enthusiastic people, from all walks of life, that it seemed no burden at all. Nevertheless, despite the growing list of requests I limited myself to just a few weekends away from home each year. A few years ago I was joined by a neighbour and teaching colleague, Bernd Weise, who has come from a similar ceramics background, to take some of the load, as offers for hosting workshops increased dramatically.

Despite the fact that many of the participants had already done research on how to build their own oven, most indicated that they would understand the process far better if they were to actually build an oven first. The format of the weekend workshop that was established in the early days seemed to be successful, and so it has continued. Two different ovens (and on rare occasions three) are constructed over the two days – a high-tech cast oven built in situ which remains with the hosts, and a low-tech clay-based oven built on a steel frame, which can be moved.

Because of the short time available in which to complete the two ovens, some components such as arches and chimney bases and steel frames are pre-made, but all the rest is constructed over the weekend.

The hosts are responsible for having the base of their high-tech oven built to their liking. They pay only for the materials used in the oven's construction, which would be equivalent to a purchased one at more than quadruple the cost. The low-tech oven is sold, usually to one of the workshop participants for less than material costs, loaded onto a trailer (sometimes a truck) by helpful participants and driven to its new owner's home.

While there are brief discussion sessions on oven design, refractory materials, construction methods and cooking tips (supported by a coloured manual), the rest is hands-on activity. While constant, the tasks are not strenuous and we have attempted to avoid using any specialist tools that would not be found in the average toolshed.

Members of a workshop group constructing a low-tech oven.

It was decided from the very first workshop that the low-tech oven should be made ready for cooking on the second day, despite the need to gradually remove the sand mould late into Saturday night and dry it out with a gas burner ready to continue with the insulation layer (while using it for cooking) on the Sunday. To spend two days building two ovens and not see one in action would be like attending a musical instrument making workshop and not hearing a note.

The great diversity of backgrounds of the participants who choose to attend the workshops is a constant surprise and delight. There are the tradesmen and DIY enthusiasts one would expect, but adding to the mix a symphony orchestra violinist, a female detective, naval commander, winemaker, nurse, food critic, doctor and any number of unrelated occupations makes for lively and enjoyable social occasions.

A high-tech oven being built at a workshop held in Red Deer, Canada.

It is hard to estimate how many participants actually go on to build their own ovens but I do get many photos sent to me of completed ovens, each one different and site specific, and often combining high-tech and low-tech characteristics. Many photos are of the newly completed oven with the proud owner/builder standing next to their creation, often with peel and pizza in hand – like a hunter standing next to a trophy kill. Many people express their wonderment that they were capable of building such an oven, never having tackled something like that before.

One week on, testing out the high-tech oven constructed at a winery workshop venue.

While names and faces may sometimes disappear from the memory, it is the amusing instances that remain. One workshop participant who had bought the low-tech oven was to travel a long distance home with the possibility of a storm brewing. After eight struggling participants had successfully loaded the oven onto his flatbed utility (pickup) I asked whether he had any protection for the oven in case it rained. He said he had a tarpaulin and would ring me when he got home. Hours later he rang to say it was the worst trip he had ever had because of his load's high centre of gravity, but reassured me that the oven had arrived safe and sound. 'Unfortunately it's covered in blue toffee,' he reported mournfully. He had used a blue plastic tarpaulin over the still-hot oven.

On another occasion husband and wife workshop participants bought the low-tech oven to take home to a nearby suburb, but did not have a lifting team to remove it from their vehicle. Annette was so keen to use her new oven, which still contained considerable heat from the afternoon's pizza session, that she put in a roast and within an hour, presto –perfectly cooked dinner!

A few days later she bribed a team of builder's labourers with a carton of beer to help shift the oven into its permanent position.

Lifting the soon-to-be blue low-tech oven onto the flatbed.

Cooking dinner on the back of a ute!

Completed high-tech oven with front ledge of local granite.

At a recent workshop a participant who decided to acquire the low the oven was asked if he had a team to lift it off when he got home. He remarked that he didn't need a team to lift it off because he had no access to the rear of his two-storey house. He had thought about this previously and the photo opposite indicates how he managed to get it into position.

For further details regarding the workshops, including photos, visit
www.woodfiredovenworkshops.com.

It's extraordinary what lengths some people will go to.

Appendix 1:
Oven Doors and Doorways

Lean-to or prop doors

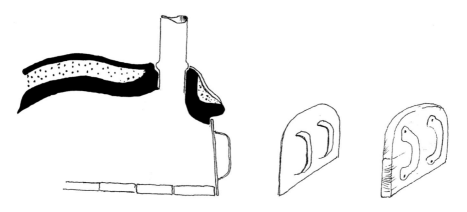

The door can be made from metal or timber. At baking temperatures wood will not ignite and, if soaked in water, will provide steam – which imparts a delightful crust to bread.

Hinge doors

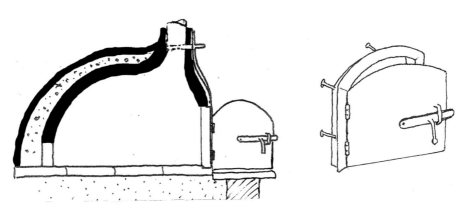

A hinged door requires a frame with 'pins' to enable it to be locked into the castable or masonry structure.

Right-angled doors

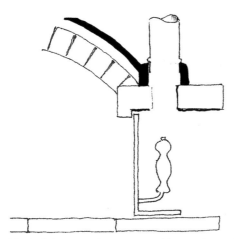

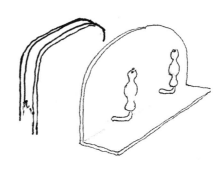

Vertical doors can be supported by a right-angle bend in the steel or attaching right-angle brackets. A double-skin door filled with insulation will retain heat.

Appendix 2:
Making Arches and Door Entries

Casting a simple arch

Step 1 Have available two thick sheets of plywood, MDF or particle board, prefereably with a melamine or sealed surface, slightly larger than the size of the required arch.

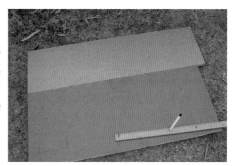

Step 2 Having determined the door size, mark the inner radius of the semi-circle to be at least 15 mm (5/8 in) inside the door radius. The outer radius can also be marked. If the arch being cast is the inner 'door stop' it is worth making the outer radius match the same radius of any outer

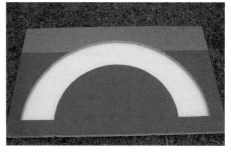

arch, be it brick or cast material. Cut out the shape thus marked from one of the sheets.

Step 3 Fasten the two sheets together. The semi-circular cut-out 'hole' created can now be lined with vertical walls of metal plate, plastic laminate or plastic garden edging of, approximately, 100 mm (4 in) height. End stops need to be incorporated to create a tight 'well' in which to pour the castable. Additional blocks may be needed to support the walls.

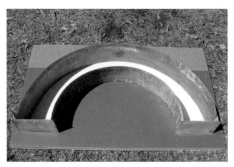

Step 4 Lightly oil the inner surfaces of the mould for easy and neat release of the finished cast. If making an inner arch, which will be subjected to the heat of the oven, mix high-temperature castable to a pourable 'porridge' state, with the addition of a handful of stainless steel 'needles', if greater strength is desired

Step 5 Make sure the mould is perfectly horizontal, then pour the castable into the mould, using a stick to spread it evenly and to remove any voids from the mix. The added vibration from a hammer drill or orbital sander placed next to the mould frame will assist in eliminating air bubbles.

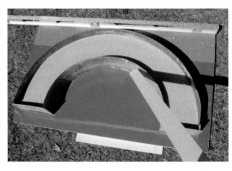

Step 6 Leave to set for at least 24 hours before shaking the cast out onto a soft surface. The downward face, which was toward the smooth, oiled surface, should be perfectly smooth and flat. It is this face that is the directed outward to take the door.

Forming a brick arch without traditional formwork

Step 1 A brick arch may be made in the horizontal position, using extruded bricks, eliminating the need to construct traditional formwork. If the outer arch is not to incorporate a chimney opening for the oven gases (that is, it is for an internal chimney oven) then it need only be of half-brick thickness. On a smooth surface lay the half-bricks evenly around a semi-circular line to form an arch of the desired dimensions.

Step 2 It is often easier to determine the outer arch dimensions first and cast or construct the back arch and door to suit. See 'Casting a simple arch' above.

Step 3 The photo shows the use of a 3-hole extruded brick of 50 mm (2 in) thickness cut in half. The thinner brick reduces the large V-shaped gaps that would be evident if using 75 mm (3 in) standard bricks. The round extrusion holes enable the use of metal reinforcing bars to be threaded through the bricks for strength.

Step 4 With bricks and reinforcing rods in place, the external gaps, end extrusion holes and any fine inner gaps can be filled with mortar. As the outer arch receives little heat from the oven there is no need for high-temperature mortar – standard Portland cement-based mortar (coloured, if desired) is satisfactory.

Step 5 Once the outer surface only is filled it can be sponged back to the brick surface. This sponging helps fill any holes that may be revealed.

Step 6 As the mortar stiffens the surface can be thoroughly cleaned back to reveal the brickwork.
[

Step 7 Once the outside mortar has set, a more fluid mix of the same mortar is poured into the wedge-shaped gaps. The mortar will flow down and around the arch, making the internal part solid and locking the reinforcing rods within the brick arch.

Step 8 The top (back of the arch) can be levelled with a trowel and left to set.

Step 9 After setting for at least 24 hours the arch can be gently slid from the smooth surface and laid on its 'back'.

Step 10 Any mortar that has crept beneath the bricks and extends over the arch surface may be brushed off using a fine wire brush.

Step 11 Any gaps that may be left can be filled with additional mortar and sponged clean to reveal the brick surface. When completely dry the arch will be strong enough to lift into place.

Step 12 If the arch is for a traditional pizza oven, with gases exiting the doorway before entering the flue hole in the arch, the arch will need to be made from full bricks. Assemble as above but leave a rectangular space in the centre (half-bricks) as a flue gap leading to the chimney.

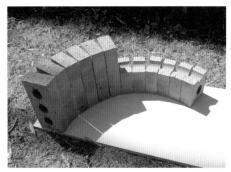

Appendix 3:
Dampers and Chimney Bases

Dampers

A sliding damper can be made from kiln shelving, often available as offcuts. It is glued together to be positioned as a complete unit.

A standard 'rain cap' (common on exhausts) makes an excellent variable damper with chain link adjustment.

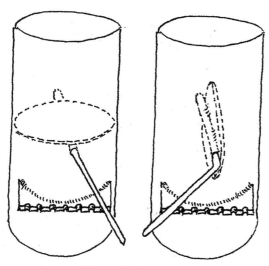

A stainless steel butterfly damper in open and shut positions. This can be fabricated within the flue pipe or as an insert.

Casting a chimney base or transition box

Step 1 To make a simple and neat base for a round stainless steel chimney all you require is a clean, round plastic bucket, a short length of pipe slightly smaller than the diameter of the chimney and a narrow roll of corrugated cardboard or similar.

Step 2 Wrap the corrugated cardboard around the short pipe till it matches the diameter of the crimped end of the stainless steel flue pipe, keeping it level with the pipe at one end. Wrap adhesive tape around the cardboard. Place the wrapped pipe in the centre of the lightly oiled bucket with the cardboard firm and even on the bottom, and hold down and in place with a brick. Pour fluid castable around the cardboard-covered pipe and allow to set.

Step 3 Once set the cast can be removed from the bucket and the inner pipe with its cardboard wrap withdrawn; it is now ready to test-fit the crimped end of the flue pipe in place. If the hole is a little tight the castable is still in a 'green' state where it can be scraped away to allow the pipe to fit.

Step 4 Where a round chimney is being fitted to a external flue opening in a traditional oven, it is usually necessary to make a 'transition' box from the rectangular opening in the arch to the round flue pipe. This view is of the underside of the box showing cardboard wrapped around a circular pipe or container.

Step 5 Instead of pouring in fluid castable, you have to line the box by hand with a stiffer mix of castable to form a 'shell' that, when inverted, will act as a manifold or transition box taking the gases from the rectangular opening to the round chimney. This box needs to be made to cover the rectangular exit opening in the door arch and should not be made too short.

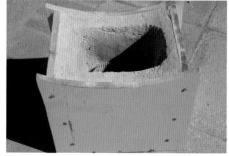

Step 6 The finished transition box ready to be mounted on top of the arch rectangular opening. You will see such a transition box in position in Chapter 5, 'Building a brick oven'.

Appendix 4:
Prospecting for and Testing Natural Clay

Step 1 Look for a likely clay source in exposed road cuttings, excavation sites or embankments. Avoid the top layer, where there may be too much organic matter.

Take a small sample of dry clay to do a field test.

All you require is a hammer or mallet, a kitchen sieve, a digging implement, a bowl and some water.

Step 2 Pound the dry clay on a solid surface to break it into a fine powder. You need only enough clay to make half a cup of sieved powder.

Step 3 Pass the crushed clay through the kitchen sieve just by shaking. Return any large lumps to be further crushed rather than trying to force them through the mesh.

Step 4 Mix a little water with the sieved clay and knead in a bowl until it is firm enough to knead between your hands. If you have added too much water, add more sieved clay until the mix stiffens.
Work the clay for a few minutes until it is not sticking to your hands.

Step 5 Roll the clay between your palms until you produce a rope-like length slightly more than pencil thickness.

Step 6 Now roll the 'rope' around your finger. If it completes a full circle without cracking, the clay is considered 'highly plastic' and particularly suitable for building an oven. If there are a few splits but the circle holds together, it is 'partially plastic' and can be used with less additional sand and stone dust, but if it breaks and falls apart, it is considered to be 'short', and you should seek another source.

Oven Building Supplies

The following generic types of supply outlets should provide you with a guide in seeking materials for building a wood fired oven. For specific suppliers in your area you are urged to search telephone directories and the internet.

Materials	Suppliers
Refractory castables, firebricks and fireclay tiles, insulating firebricks and boards, refractory cements and mortars, ceramic blanket, ceramic tubes, stainless steel 'needles', kiln shelving (for dampers)	Refractory specialists, refractory and ceramics suppliers, some pottery suppliers
AAC blocks (Hebel, Xella, Eco)	Insulating building suppliers (seek trade names)
Perlite and vermiculite	Hydroponic suppliers, spray insulation specialists
Temperature probes	Temperature control companies, pizza supply specialists, some caterers' suppliers
Stainless steel flues	Stove suppliers, some hardware stores
Rain caps (for dampers)	Exhaust suppliers, truck specialists
Standard clay bricks, pavers and tiles	Brick and paver manufacturers, brick and paver retail stores, paver and tile stores, some outdoor garden suppliers
Decomposed granite (granitic sand) or gravel, concrete blocks, sand, cement (Portland, standard, builders), cement colours and waterproofing	Sand, stone and gravel outlets, landscape suppliers, garden suppliers, hardware stores
Powdered clay	Mineral suppliers, pottery suppliers
Steel (for oven base frames and doors)	Steel suppliers and fabricators
Sheet metal	Metal fabricators
Particle board (MDF, chipboard) and plywood (for mould making)	Hardware stores, joineries and kitchen bench makers (for off-cuts or scrap)
Pizza tools	Pizza supply specialists, caterers' suppliers

Glossary

Air-setting mortar A prepared mixture, usually containing, high-temperature cement, clay, alumina powder and sodium silicate. It is normally made to a paste consistency. Sets hard when exposed to the air.

Barrel arch A continuous curved arch form with parallel straight sides.

Brickies sand A fine sand with enough clay content to enable it to hold together when moist. Favoured by bricklayers.

Castable An industry term referring to a high temperature concrete made from high-alumina cement and a variety of high-alumina aggregates. Made in many grades.

Ceramic blanket A blanket-like material, with excellent insulating properties, made from silica and alumina. These two ingredients are melted at extremely high temperatures in an electric arc furnace and the molten material is air blown to create fine threads from which the ceramic fibre blanket is made.

Crusher dust The finest aggregate produced by the crushing of stone for road and concrete requirements. Also called stone dust, cracker dust, packing stone dust.

Decomposed granite A gravel-like material resulting from the weathering and decomposition of granite, usually beneath the ground. It has a considerable amount of clay among the silica pebbles that enables it to be packed tightly. Sometimes called granitic sand or granitic gravel.

Hearth The floor or sole of the oven.

Heat bank A dense mass of solid brick, rammed rubble (gravel, decomposed granite or similar material) that is used beneath the oven floor to retain the heat in the oven for a prolonged period.

High-temperature cement A cement capable of withstanding high temperatures made from heating a combination of alumina and calcium. Ciment Fondu® is a popular brand of high-temperature cement.

High-temperature mortar A variety of mixtures are produced, usually containing high temperature cement, fired (or calcined) high-alumina aggregate or ceramic material (grog), often with some fireclay as a plasticiser.

Traditional mortars have simply been fireclay or kaolin (a pure form of clay) where joints are thin, or a weak hydrated lime, Portland cement and sand mix in the proportion 1 : 1 : 9.

Hot face The inner layer of the oven closest to the heat.

Lean-to door A doorway cover, usually of metal or wood, that leans against the oven opening.

Masonry block A concrete building block manufactured as a solid or cavity form. .

Paver A fired clay thin brick designed for paved areas. Sometimes called 'clay paver' as opposed to 'concrete paver'.

Peel A flat shovel-like device for placing and removing pizzas and breads from ovens. A thin metal peel is generally used for pizza, a wooden peel for bread.

Perlite A pumice-like material manufactured from heating naturally occurring perlite rock (a volcanic glass) so that it expands considerably. An excellent insulator.

Prop door An oven entrance cover with a right-angle bottom plate that allows it to remain in a vertical position.

Refractory Material which will withstand high temperatures.

Scuffle A damp mop of fibres or cloth that is used to remove fine ash from the oven floor.

Sodium silicate Also known as waterglass. It is a clear, fluid, waterproofing and binding agent that can withstand high temperatures. Made by combining various silica sands with soda ash (sodium carbonate).

Spall To flake or fragment.

Stainless steel 'needles' Short, fine 'chopped' lengths of stainless steel used in the furnace industries to reinforce high-temperature castable cement mixes.

Trammel A gauge from a fixed central point on the oven floor used for creating a hemispherical dome.

Vermiculite A very light insulating material made from heating a mica-like silica to expand its size 22 times.

Bibliography

Bacon, Richard M. *The Forgotten Art of Building and Using a Brick Bake Oven: How to Date, Renovate or Use an Existing Brick Oven, or to Construct a New One*, Alan C. Hood & Co., Chambersburg, PA, 1977.

Bell, Peter. 'Chinese Ovens on Mining Sites in Australia', in P. Macgregor (ed.), *Histories of the Chinese in Australasia and the South Pacific*, Museum of Chinese Australian History, Melbourne, 1995, pp. 213–29.

Boily, Lise & Jean-François Blanchette. *The Bread Ovens of Quebec*, National Museums of Canada, Ottawa, 1979.

Cardew, Michael. *Pioneer Pottery*, Longmans, Green & Co., London, 1969.

Carpenter, Anna. *The Ultimate Wood-fired Oven Book*, Schiffer, Atglen, PA, 2008.

Culver, C.C. *The Settlement of Yandoit Creek & The Gervasonis*, Jim Crow Creek Press, Daylesford, VIC, 2003.

Denzer, Kiko. *Build Your Own Earth Oven: A Low-Cost Wood-Fired Mud Oven; Simple Sourdough Bread; Perfect Loaves*, HandPrint Press, Blodgett, OR, 2004.

Gray, Alan (ed.). *Back Yard Ovens, Vol 1*, Earth Garden Books, Trentham, VIC, 2007.

Gray, Alan (ed.). *Back Yard Ovens, Vol 2*, Earth Garden Books, Trentham, VIC, 2010.

Gray, Alan (ed.). *Wood Oven Recipes*, Earth Garden Books, Trentham, VIC, 2009.

Jaine, Tom. *Building a Wood-fired Oven for Bread and Pizza*, Prospect Books, Devon, UK, 1996.

Jeavons, Russell. *Your Brick Oven: Building It and Baking in It*, Grub Street, London, 2005.

Karlin, Mary. *Wood-Fired Cooking*, Ten Speed Press, Berkeley, CA, 2009.

Mugnaini, Andrea. *The Art of Wood Fired Cooking*, Gibbs Smith, Layton, UT, 2010.

Riccio, Ben. *Pizza From Naples*, New Holland Publishing, Sydney, 2010.

Scheele, Charel. *Adobe Oven for Old World Breads: Bread Cook Book*, Writers Club Press, Lincoln, NE, 2002.

Wegars, Priscilla. 'Who's Been Working on the Railroad?', *Historical Archeology* 25, 1, 1991, pp. 37–60.

Wing, Daniel & Alan Scott. *The Bread Builders: Hearth Loaves and Masonry Ovens*, Chelsea Green Publishing, White River Junction, VT, 1999.

Index